Polar
Explorers
for
Kids

Polar Explorers *for* Kids

Historic Expeditions
to the Arctic and Antarctic
with 21 Activities

Maxine Snowden

CHICAGO
REVIEW
PRESS

Library of Congress Cataloging-in-Publication Data

Snowden, Maxine.

    Polar explorers for kids : historic expeditions to the Arctic and
Antarctica with 21 activities / Maxine Snowden.   p. cm.

    Summary: Describes the travels and adventures of Arctic and Antarctic explorers through-
out history, from Erik the Red in 981 or 982 to Gretel Ehrlich in 2000.

Includes bibliographical references and index.

ISBN 978-1-55652-500-1

    1. Explorers—Polar regions—Biography—Juvenile literature.   2. Polar regions—
Discovery and exploration—Juvenile literature.   3. Polar regions—Study and teaching—
Activity programs—Juvenile literature.   [1. Explorers—Polar regions.   2. Polar regions—
Discovery and exploration.]   I. Title.

G634.S66 2003   919.804′092′2—dc21   2003004379

Acknowledgments

This book would not be possible without the valuable contributions of Rita Baladad, Catherine
Bosin, Victor Croft, Laura D'Argo, Allison Felus, David Gebhart, Linda Gray, Jason Groom,
Sara Hoerdeman, Gerilee Hundt, Bruce Koon, Robert Koon, Jeff Marek, Linda Matthews,
Amber McKown, Jason Muse, Mark Noble, Jerome Pohlen, Scott Rattray, Lisa Rosenthal,
Cynthia Sherry, Jef Smith, and Stefanie Solomon.

Cover image credits: Clockwise: Roald Amundsen's ship the *Gjoa*, Vancouver Maritime Museum;
polar bear, PhotoDisc, Inc.; from F. A. Cook's expedition, State Library of South Australia;
penguins, PhotoDisc, Inc.; sextant, Vancouver Maritime Museum; Commander Robert E. Peary,
National Archives; puffin, Carry Given Photography
Cover and interior design: Rattray Design
Interior illustrations: Laura D'Argo

Note to Readers

IN THIS BOOK you will find dates on which various expeditions launched, numbers of men who were on them, and accounts of what happened on an explorer's first voyage (as opposed to his second or third). There are many reliable sources of information (although, unfortunately, the actual journals of many of these explorers are out of print), but inconsistencies do exist in various accounts: for example, even the birth years of some of the earlier explorers are not known with certainty. In writing this book, I have made every effort to present the most accurate information available.

Contents

Introduction

For centuries, people have been fascinated by the exquisite icy wildernesses of the Arctic and Antarctic. While both areas captured the imagination of explorers, each land mass has its own distinct characteristics and appeal. The Arctic, where the North Pole is found, has polar bears, but no penguins. Antarctica, home of the South Pole, has penguins, but no polar bears. The Arctic has land around and under some—but not all—of its ice. Antarctica is just a giant slab of glacial ice over rock, and it has active volcanoes. Both poles are such powerful "engines" for cold-air patterns and cold-water currents that they affect the climate of the whole planet. Thousands of people inhabit the Arctic—and have for many thousands of years. Antarctica, with its harsher climate, has no native peoples, but hundreds of scientists have spent months at a time here to study this vast and treacherous glacial wonderland.

Over the years, technological advances such as navigational devices, protective clothing, and sturdier vessels have made exploration of these distant lands slightly less daunting. But even just a few decades ago, staggering dangers, difficulties, and discomforts awaited polar explorers in the Arctic and Antarctica. These adventurers braved deadly weather with poor maps, imperfect navigation technology, impossible communication challenges, dangerous animals, uncertain food supplies, and, often, ill health. Explorers faced unending danger and fear—one storm could shove enough ice at a wooden ship to crush it like a piece of hard candy between your jaws. One summer day's sail through a field of icebergs could panic an inexperienced crew into mutiny. An early winter could strand an expedition on an ice floe (a large slab of floating ice), a potentially fatal place. A single mistake could end the whole venture, and unsuccessful explorers might not be given more money from benefactors to attempt any more excursions.

Why did they do it? Why did the polar explorers set their dreams for farthest north and farthest south? Their reasons varied. A few early adventurers were hermits seeking a place to be alone with God, or were simply curious about what was, at the time, believed to be a green and pleasant place. Others sought to be the first to find a new land, or to thread a northwest passage from Europe to the Orient through the Arctic, which would allow for trade and create a dramatic global reach for the explorers' societies. Some wanted to be the first to map the coast of Antarctica or to cross it on land. Still others were motivated primarily by fame and the titles and riches it could bring; monarchs knighted quite a few of the earlier explorers in the early days, and later explorers sought the vast and frenzied media exposure that often followed a first-ever accomplishment. Some explorers wanted to claim a land base in Antarctica or to win an international race to the North or South Pole for their homeland. Many simply loved making scientific discoveries: they wanted to observe the penguins on an Antarctic island, to invent a new navigational device, to study polar bears and other animals in the Arctic, or to explore the customs and activities of the Inuit (formerly called Eskimos) who inhabited the land. And of course, some were motivated by possible fortune; these explorers sought to claim natural resources including new whaling grounds, gold and amber in the north, and oil and gas reserves in the south. No matter what their motivation was, however, all of their ventures to these mysterious lands were exciting, dangerous, and full of possibilities.

The polar regions have attracted a chilled parade of explorers from many countries for more than a thousand years. *Polar Explorers for Kids* will introduce you to many of these extraordinary adventurers, to the wonders that are known about the incredible lands they explored, and to the mysteries that have yet to be solved by future explorers—maybe you!

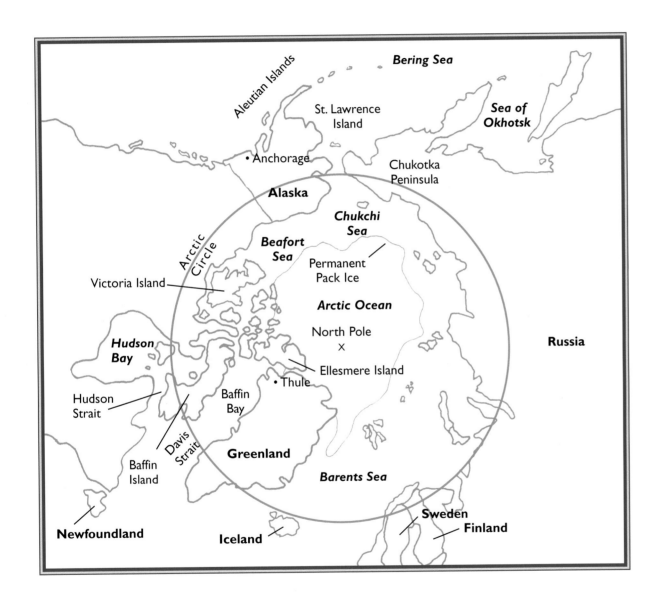

Bering Sea

Aleutian Islands

St. Lawrence
Island

Sea of
Okhotsk

• Anchorage

Chukotka
Peninsula

Alaska

Chukchi
Sea

Beafort
Sea

Permanent
Pack Ice

Arctic Circle

Victoria Island

Arctic Ocean

North Pole
X

Russia

Hudson
Bay

Ellesmere Island

• Thule

Hudson
Strait

Baffin
Bay

Davis Strait

Baffin
Island

Greenland

Barents Sea

Newfoundland

Iceland

Sweden

Finland

Part I

The Arctic

Arctic Exploration Time Line

~5000 B.C. Inuit people (formerly called "Eskimos") establish themselves in the Arctic region

A.D. 860–870 Vikings discover and settle Iceland

981–986 Erik the Red locates and settles Greenland

1001 Leif Eriksson (Erik the Red's son) explores Baffin Island, Labrador, and Newfoundland

~1272 Marco Polo explores China

1492 Christopher Columbus explores the West Indies and the New World

1497 John Cabot discovers Newfoundland

Europeans begin to contemplate creating a "Northwest Passage," a route to China through the Arctic

1498 Christopher Columbus explores South America

1500 João Fernandes reaches Greenland

Gaspar Corte Real reaches Newfoundland, kidnaps 57 Indians, and takes them back to Portugal

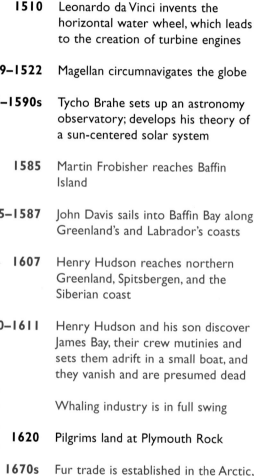

1510 Leonardo da Vinci invents the horizontal water wheel, which leads to the creation of turbine engines

1519–1522 Magellan circumnavigates the globe

1575–1590s Tycho Brahe sets up an astronomy observatory; develops his theory of a sun-centered solar system

1585 Martin Frobisher reaches Baffin Island

1585–1587 John Davis sails into Baffin Bay along Greenland's and Labrador's coasts

1607 Henry Hudson reaches northern Greenland, Spitsbergen, and the Siberian coast

1610–1611 Henry Hudson and his son discover James Bay, their crew mutinies and sets them adrift in a small boat, and they vanish and are presumed dead

Whaling industry is in full swing

1620 Pilgrims land at Plymouth Rock

1670s Fur trade is established in the Arctic, joining whaling, sealing, and cod fishery industries

1740   Vitus Bering discovers Alaska across the Bering Strait from Russia

1776   United States Declaration of Independence is signed

1785   Russia settles the Aleutian Islands, between mainland Russia and Alaska

1819   William Parry passes Greenland into Lancaster Sound, then travels north of the North Magnetic Pole; spends the winter near Melville Island

1845–1847   Sir John Franklin reaches the Victoria Strait and maps miles of island coastline; he and his entire crew vanish

1861–1865   United States Civil War

1882–1883   First International Polar Year; 11 countries participate in studies of the Arctic and Antarctica

❖1879   Thomas A. Edison perfects the electric lightbulb

1880s   Inupiats discover oil seeping from the ground near the Beaufort Sea

1893–1896   Fridtjof Nansen analyzes polar water currents; uses them to move his ship to "farthest north"

1903   Wright Brothers first fly an airplane at Kitty Hawk, North Carolina

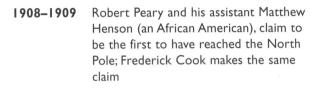

1908–1909   Robert Peary and his assistant Matthew Henson (an African American), claim to be the first to have reached the North Pole; Frederick Cook makes the same claim

1908–1918   Vilhjalmur Stefansson discovers and re-maps huge areas of Arctic; promotes a natural gas industry and oxen ranching for Arctic peoples

1914–1918   World War I

1939–1945   World War II

1955   Louise Arner Boyd, a photographer, becomes the first woman to reach the North Pole by plane

1962   John Glenn, Jr., becomes the first American astronaut to orbit Earth

1968   Huge oil deposits are found in Alaska's Prudhoe Bay area

1986   William Steger and Paul Schurke reach the North Pole by dogsled

   Ann Bancroft becomes the first woman to reach the North Pole by land

1991   Nunavut, a circumpolar province within Canada, is established

1993–2000   Gretel Ehrlich, a writer, explores Greenland and its native peoples

~ indicates approximate date

1

Erik the Red Reaches Greenland, 981 or 982

Y ou might think that the first person to lay claim to land in the majestic Arctic would be a gallant hero—a nobleman in search of glory for his king, maybe, or a scientist on a quest for discovery and knowledge. That is not the case, however. The person credited with first settling territory in the Arctic was actually a bloodthirsty killer who discovered Greenland, a part of the Arctic, while running for his life.

Erik the Red was a Viking. The Vikings were an aggressive group of Scandinavian explorers and warriors who plundered the coasts of Europe in the eighth to tenth centuries. Even by Viking standards, Erik the Red was considered a particularly nasty person, and he was exiled from his native country of Norway after committing murders,

Puffins nest in underground burrows on the tops of sea cliffs in Greenland.

according to the Graenlendinga Saga, a medieval Icelandic chronicle. Upon his exile, Erik settled in Iceland with his father, Thorvald. But his taste for blood didn't stop. He murdered two more men in Iceland, which earned him a three-year sentence of outlawry. In the 900s Iceland had no prisons; the punishment for murder was banishment from "civilized" society. Those who were outlawed were forced to surrender their farms and most of their other possessions and run away to far-off places, where they tried to hide until their sentence was up (according to the law, anyone who could find them during the years of their sentence could kill them). Some outlaws left Iceland only to sneak back into mainland Scandinavia. Some hid out in caves or secluded sheds on small, uninhabited islands, but the long winters took most of their lives. Erik the Red decided to find a new country instead.

The year was either 981 or 982—historians are not sure of the date. After his sentence, Erik the Red quickly found a temporary hiding place on Oxen Island, a very small island in one of Iceland's west-coast bays. He chose this place because the dangerous tidal whirlpools that surround it can swallow a small boat, and he thought that they would protect him from those seeking revenge. Here, with a few allies, he gathered supplies, readied a sturdy boat, and made plans to head off to uncharted territory.

As far back as the early 800s, the Vikings were masters of shipbuilding, and they used their boats to conduct pirate raids upon coastal farms, towns, and churches all over the northern world and as far away as Russia and Turkey. The *knörrs*, or boats, they built were made of wood. The planks of the knörrs were caulked and treated with animal hair or wool, which was heated until it was almost like tar, then smeared onto the wood to seal it. The *keel* (the main structural part of a boat, which extends down into the water from the boat's bottom) of a Viking ship was not only long, but was made of one piece of wood so that it was especially strong. This made the ship easier to steer, as did the *steerboard*, a rudder that extended out from the right side of the ship. (The modern word *starboard* comes from this word.) The Vikings' boats had sails, but they were also outfitted with oars to use as a backup. The ships were about 76 feet long and about 17 feet across at the widest point. They required only six feet of water in order to float, making it easy to approach close to shore. Each boat carried a crew of about 35 people on warfaring voyages, but the ships carried more people on journeys of exploration such as Erik the Red's. A Viking ship could also carry 30 tons of cargo. Every night a tent was strung up over much of the boat so that people could sleep under a shelter.

Viking explorers such as Erik the Red had no maps of their routes, no charts of ocean depth or ocean currents, and no compasses to aid them on their journeys. Yet the Vikings

Early Ideas About the Arctic

From 330 B.C. to A.D. 800 and beyond, many people in the Mediterranean countries of Europe believed that the Arctic was a land of evil-tempered people who had the nature of bears and who lived near an ocean swirling with dangerous whirlpools. It was also believed, however, that hidden beyond the polar coasts was a graceful land where the flowing water sounded like music and vines bore fruit 12 times a year. They called this magical place the Land of the Hyperboreans. Of course, no one had ever been to this imaginary land, nor did they know anyone who had. Erik the Red decided to be the first to venture there and come back alive.

The Vikings of Iceland knew all the old stories of a new land to the west. Almost 100 years before Erik the Red set sail for it, the Viking Gunnbjorn Ulfsson was blown off course in a storm and saw a vast land in the distance. Although he did not get very close to it, he claimed that this was the enchanted place that the stories described. A few years after that, another Viking tried to spend the winter on the east coast of this new land after being caught there in another storm. He disappeared without a trace, and for almost a century, no Viking went there again.

navigated all over the northern world and beyond.

How did Erik the Red navigate his way without getting lost or going in circles? He used several subtle techniques. To avoid getting lost on the trackless ocean, he always tried to sail in a straight line. On clear days, the Vikings used the sun to accomplish this. In the northernmost part of the world, mid-May through mid-August has always been the favorite time to undertake explorations, because during this summer season it never gets dark. For this reason, the region is called "the Land of the Midnight Sun." Icelanders used this to their advantage on journeys. They also knew where the sun was positioned in the sky at noon in their homeland, and they used that knowledge to steer their ships, keeping the sun at that same height and adjusting their course every day at noon.

On cloudy days the Vikings looked for land-dwelling birds to guide them to shore. If there were any such birds in the vicinity of the boat (the Vikings knew which birds lived on shore and which lived out on the open ocean), the Vikings could follow them to land as they flew home each evening. This method has its limits, however; it only works relatively close to land, and it does not work at all in the spring and fall migration seasons, when shorebirds do not fly back and forth to land daily. But the Vikings were natural observers of their environments,

What Are Latitude and Longitude?

Thousands of years ago, people developed a way of using imaginary horizontal and vertical lines to identify the location of any place or Earth. The horizontal imaginary lines are called *parallels*, or lines of latitude. The vertical imaginary lines are called *meridians*, or lines of longitude.

Think of the Earth as a big orange, with the North Pole at the top, where the stem is, and the South Pole at the bottom. Now imagine a horizontal line that goes all the way around the middle of the Earth. This line is called the *equator*, and it divides the Earth into two halves—the northern hemisphere and the southern hemisphere. Anything in the northern hemisphere (north of the equator) has a north latitude, and anything in the southern hemisphere (south of the equator) has a south latitude.

The distance between the equator and each of the poles is divided into segments called *degrees*. Degrees can be divided into smaller segments called *minutes*. And minutes can be divided into even smaller segments called *seconds*. There are 90 degrees between the equator and each of the poles. The equator is at 0 degrees, which means that the North Pole is 90 degrees north of it (90 degrees north latitude) and the South Pole is 90 degrees south of it (90 degrees south latitude).

If you were at 89 degrees north latitude, how close to the North Pole would you be? Very close! If you were at 89 degrees 22 minutes north latitude, you'd be even closer. At 89 degrees 22 minutes 5 seconds north latitude, you'd be just a tiny bit closer still.

Just as we use imaginary horizontal lines to determine latitude, we use imaginary vertical lines or meridians, around the earth to determine longitude. The Prime Meridian is the imaginary line that runs vertically around the middle of the earth. Its location is 0 degrees longitude. Meridians go from 0 to 180 degrees east, and then to 180 degrees west. This gives a total range of 360 degrees, a full circle.

By using both lines of latitude and longitude, you can pinpoint the exact location of any place on the Earth. How do you do this? In the early days, explorers found their latitude by measuring the position of the sun, the North Star, or another star in relation to the horizon. Longitude was measured using instruments such as the *chronometer*, which keeps time with great accuracy. Today we have something called a Global Positioning System, which uses satellite signals to pinpoint the latitude and longitude of any position on the planet.

Arctic Migrations

People aren't the only animals that have left the Arctic when winter approached. Several species of whales, such as the gray whale, migrate out of the Arctic for winter as well. The most amazing mass migrations are those of the birds. A few small Arctic or subarctic islands can be home to hundreds of thousands of nesting cormorants (black birds that are about a foot tall) or kittiwake (cliff-dwelling gulls) during the summer, and then none during the winter as these birds migrate south.

The longest migration belongs to the Arctic tern, whose nickname could be "the bird allergic to darkness." This gray and white bird features a long white forked tail, a red beak, and a black "racing stripe" on its head. Arctic terns migrate to the Arctic and subarctic during these areas' summer months, when the sun never sets. They then migrate to Antarctica for its summer (the northern world's winter), again living in a land of neverending sun. In just one year, an Arctic tern will fly between 22,000 and 25,000 miles in its round-trip migration.

Kittiwake gulls nest on the rocky ledges of sea cliffs in Greenland.

and they knew that on cloudy days they could also look for *iceblink*, a faint yellowish or greenish haze that appears on the underside of clouds in the far distance. A yellowish haze was the reflection up onto the clouds of a vast area of snow or ice; a greenish haze was the reflection of land. Spotting iceblink requires keen attention, but once the greenish haze was seen, the Vikings could steer toward it.

At night, Erik the Red used the North Star to navigate, again using the principle of staying on a straight route over the open ocean. This is the only star in the northern hemisphere that does not appear to move from our vantage point on Earth: all the other stars in the constellations appear to swing in a circular pattern, slightly shifting their positions each night. The Vikings knew where the North Star was located in the sky above Iceland, and they looked to it to keep to their course. Storms could blow them hundreds of miles off a straight course, and it often took many days to get back to where they wanted to be, but they always knew in what direction to head. In the process, they often found lands they would not otherwise have come across.

Embarking on his quest to find the mysterious land he'd heard so much about, Erik the Red decided on a single navigational method: keeping the Snaefellsnes Glacier, on Iceland's west coast, directly behind his ship. This very tall glacier is shaped like a cone and reflects light well, making its iceblink distinct for at least 100 miles. It is still used to help determine direction today.

After sailing for about 500 miles across the North Atlantic, Erik the Red reached the east coast of an unknown territory. Finding no good place to land, Erik continued around the southern tip and up the west coast, and eventually sailed into one of Greenland's many *fjords*. A fjord is a narrow, deep inlet of the sea that runs between cliffs or glaciers. As Erik the Red glided through the fjord he saw that, although a glacier stretched high on both sides of the fjord as far as one could see, sloping up to it were large, beautiful green fields. The fjord itself was rich in fish, seals, and walruses. Erik liked what he saw, decided to stay, and immediately named the fjord after himself: "Eiriksfjord."

The first thing Erik and his crew did was unpack extra sleeping bags, which were made out of animal skins. They'd need to sleep with the furry side close to their bodies if they wanted to stay warm—and alive—in this vast, chilly, and empty place. Although other northern people created similar devices to stay warm, the Vikings are credited with having invented the sleeping bag,

Make a Viking Compass

Unlike today's explorers who set out for distant lands, the Vikings discovered the New World without using a Global Positioning System (GPS), computers, or even motors on their ships. They used *compasses*, devices that are used for determining direction by means of a magnetic needle that always points north. The Vikings constructed compasses using naturally magnetic rocks called *lodestones*, which are rich in the mineral magnetite. These magnetic rocks are attracted to the Earth's own magnetic core, causing them to point north.

1. Fill the bucket about three-fourths full of water.
2. Float the piece of wood in the water. Place the lodestone on the wood, making sure that it doesn't sink.
3. Several feet away from the bucket (to protect against the two magnets interfering with each other), use the regular compass to locate due north. Now look at the direction in which the lodestone is aligned. Is it the same?

Materials

Wooden bucket (or a bucket made of another nonmagnetic material, such as plastic or glass)

Small piece of flat, lightweight wood (it should be large

enough for the lodestone to be placed on it, but small enough to float in the bucket)

Lodestone (see note)

Regular compass to use for comparison purposes

---

4. Do you think it might sometimes be more convenient or practical to have a lodestone instead of a regular compass to determine location? In what instances?

Note: Lodestones are available at most science stores and at some rock shops. They may be purchased from Edmund Scientifics via the company's Web site (www.scientificsonline.com) or by telephone (800-728-6999).

and they used them on ships as well as on land.

Erik's next step was to name the country. He chose to call it Greenland—a deliberate advertisement. He wanted his fellow Icelanders to think about the land's green fields, so that some would want to settle there with him. (Those who eventually did were surprised to discover that 95 percent of Greenland is actually *white*,

The Runic Alphabet

The Vikings used the runic alphabet, which consisted of a set of characters called *runes*. The origin of this alphabet is traced back to the early years of the first century A.D., and its popularity spread as the Vikings and other northern tribes roamed across Europe, Russia, and Greenland. It was commonly used in Europe throughout the Middle Ages (800 to 1500), and even later in Scandinavia

Many tribes, including the Goths, Vandals, Lombards, Franks, Frisians, Teutons, Angles, Saxons, Jutes, and Scandinavians, used their own versions of the runic alphabet. They "wrote" by carving the runes into wood, rocks, animal skins, and metals. Runes are made of vertical strokes (that go against a wood's grain, if wood is used as a tablet) and other straight lines on a slant. Horizontal strokes are not used, as it would be difficult to distinguish them from the natural grain of a wood tablet. In addition, runes are not made using circles or half circles, the way some of our own alphabet letters are, because those shapes are not easy to carve.

Runic writing was used for many things, including marking ownership. The small slats shown in this picture were attached to objects, much as we attach luggage tags to suitcases today. Runes also appeared on coins, jewelry, rocks, and other directional markers (one might write on a boulder "we went north from here"), and gravestones. Some were elaborate messages to and from kings or other leaders; others were like graffiti, written just for fun.

To date, about 5,000 runic inscriptions have been found. Many others, however, have been forever lost—especially those carved into wood, which decays (the wood pieces might also have been used for kindling once the message was conveyed). The greatest number of runic inscriptions have been found on large rocks in the upland area of Sweden.

Scholars sometimes find the runes hard to understand. For example, one thick gold necklace, found in what is now Romania, bears the inscription *gutaniowihailag*. They know that *gutani* was the name of a local tribe among the Goths. They also realize that *hailag* means holy. Scholars suspect that the "o" is short for *opala*, which means the owner, but they are uncertain about what the "wi" signified.

as it is covered in snow and ice.) Erik's plan was to explore the new land during his period of outlawry and then, once his three-year sentence was up, to go back and recruit Icelanders to join him in claiming the territory and settling in Greenland.

It's not clear whether the Inuit, who are native to the Arctic, inhabited this southern part of the land during this time or later migrated to Greenland from the north; if they were in the area, however, they certainly hid well. During the three winters and two summers that he explored Greenland while waiting out his sentence, Erik the Red apparently saw no native peoples on the land. As far as he was concerned, this "new" land was free for the taking—and he intended to take as much as he could. When his sentence was over Erik returned to Iceland. He described Greenland in glowing terms, and he found families looking for new land. His own family, including his son Leif Eriksson (who would later discover America—about 400 years before Christopher Columbus), joined him in moving to Greenland. In 25 ships an unknown number of people loaded their tools and other possessions, including their sheep, cows, goats, and pigs. The ships set sail in the spring of 985 or 986. Fierce storms battered them along the way. Several ships sank; others turned around and headed back home. Only 14 of the 25 ships reached Greenland. They held about 450 people, including Erik the Red.

Build a Snow Cave

When the Viking families first arrived in Greenland, they slept on their boats until they could build houses. But during their initial stay in Greenland, Erik the Red and his crew almost certainly built and slept in snow caves to protect themselves from the cold. If you are stuck outdoors in a blizzard, a snow cave can save your life.

1. Using the shovels, pile snow into a huge mound that is at least eight feet high, six feet long, and six feet wide. (This amount, once compressed, will make a snow cave big enough for two).
2. Let the mound of snow sit overnight. This is absolutely necessary to make the snow harder and more solid: gravity will pull the snow down toward the bottom of the mound, collapsing air pockets between the flakes. If this step is not taken, the roof may collapse later.
3. The next day, slap the snow with the flat part of the shovel to pack it even tighter. You want it to be as solid as the hardest-packed snowball. Start by slapping the top, then work on all the sides, and then do the top again. When you're finished you should have a very compact mound.
4. Use smaller shovels and your glove-covered hands to dig out snow from one of the sides to form the cave. Keep the opening small so that the inside will be cozy; the real purpose of a snow cave is to protect people from blizzards and subzero temperatures. It is *very important* to keep the roof and each side at least two feet

thick. This will prevent them from collapsing. Have an adult check this in at least five places on the roof and sides by shoving the yardstick two feet in from the outside, making sure that it can't be seen on the inside.
5. Once the walls and roof have been checked and the adult who is assisting says it's OK, you can just crawl in.
6. If you want to, you can decorate your snow cave. You might want to give it a name, with the letters (maybe runes?) made out of sticks or just gouged into the snow. You can push dried leaves or evergreen boughs into the top and the outside walls for a camouflaged look. Add a flag if you like. You can also place a washable rug on the floor of your snow cave.

Depending on the temperature outside, a snow cave can last for an hour or for months. Have an adult check the roof and walls often to make sure they're solid and still two feet thick. And keep the neighborhood dogs and raccoons out!

Erik and his family settled at Brattahlid, the name he gave to his farm on Eiriksfjord, where they built a sturdy house made of thick rocks covered with sod, and a barn that held 40 cattle. Some of the people who had traveled to Greenland with Erik claimed land in the same area and built 189 other small farmsteads. The rest of the Viking group continued almost 200 miles farther up the west coast and established a second settlement in an area that Erik had explored earlier. Here there was room for 90 more farms on the coast, before the land became completely covered by the layers of thick ice and snow called the Greenland ice pack.

The Viking civilization in Greenland flourished from the late 900s until the late 1100s, with Erik the Red and his descendants thriving on his original fjord. At its peak, the two Greenland settlements had 3,000 inhabitants. They grew grasses for hay, and the livestock they had brought with them provided meat as well as milk, cheese, and other dairy products. But they needed to trade with Iceland and other northern European countries to get wheat and other grains, metal, and tools.

During their time in Greenland, the Vikings continued to explore the Arctic and sub-Arctic, often looking for timber and other materials to trade. (Iceland, their trading partner, has almost no trees.) Among them two explorers stand out: Leif Eriksson (Erik's son) and Bjarni Herjulfsson. As described in the medieval Icelandic sagas, Leif

A statue of Leif Ericksson, who explored the New World, in downtown Reykjavík, Iceland.

explored the Arctic and sub-Arctic, perhaps as far west as Maine or Nova Scotia (a place they called Vinland because of the wild grapes that grew there), but certainly into Newfoundland, where a Viking base camp has been excavated by scientists. Now called L'Anse aux Meadows, this settlement on the shores of northern Newfoundland includes eight Viking houses. Evidence indicates that the area was inhabited until about 1014. In the course of their Arctic explorations, the Vikings also reached close to 76 degrees north, a record that lasted about 250 years.

Until the 1100s, ships sailed to and from Greenland without encountering much ocean ice or many icebergs. But, by the end of the 1100s, the climate started to grow colder. The Greenland ice pack grew thicker and wider, coming closer to the Vikings' homes. The ice on the fjord didn't break up until midsummer. Fall came earlier and spring came later, shortening the growing season for hay. This meant that less livestock could be supplied with enough of it to survive the very long winter. Fewer ships from Europe sailed through the now-dangerous iceberg obstacle course. No one wanted to risk pushing his ship's wooden hull through the deadly pack ice (sea ice that has formed into a large mass) near the shore.

This climate trend continued. By the 1200s it was even colder, and even fewer ships arrived with supplies. Then, in 1349, the Black Death

Climate Change

Modern scientists have analyzed the climate in Greenland and elsewhere by drilling deep into Greenland's glacier ice and by analyzing the thickness of tree rings (a sign of robust growth) across the northern hemisphere. They have discovered that the period from the late 800s through the 1100s was unusually warm. The reasons for this medieval warm period are largely unknown, but it is clear that human activity had nothing to do with the changes. One theory cites a possible slight wobble or change in the tilt of the Earth's axis, the point around which our planet spins. Another mentions a possible change in the sun's output of solar energy. Either of these would affect the strength of the sun that reaches the Arctic.

As the warm period ended, Europe entered an era called the Little Ice Age—temperatures became a couple of degrees cooler on average. This is when the Vikings in Greenland encountered their hardships. Today's climate in Greenland is close to the climate that destroyed the Viking civilization, but temperatures are beginning to warm again. This time the cause is, at least in part, human activity. Consumption of oil, gasoline, and other chemicals has damaged the *ozone layer* (the layer in the atmosphere that blocks most solar ultraviolet radiation from entry into the lower atmosphere), resulting in *global warming*, an increase in the average temperature of the planet.

who had resided in the north, began to migrate farther south in search of warmer climes. They were not happy to encounter the fierce Vikings, and the two groups frequently battled. The Thule Inuit were hunters, not farmers, which gave them an advantage over their new neighbors, since the Vikings' livestock, like the Vikings themselves, increasingly did not have enough to eat. They were also good fighters, using "bombs" made of moose bladders to knock the Vikings down in battles. The Vikings had no guns and were weakened by malnutrition. In 1379 the Inuit killed 18 Vikings and took two boys captive. By 1410 both Viking settlements faced extinction as deaths continued to mount.

Although the Vikings were clearly the first group of people to find the New World, they did not permanently colonize it. By 1500, the Viking civilization of Greenland had weakened so much that it simply vanished. Visitors today can still see the ruins of Erik the Red's house on the west Greenland fjord.

plague that had already blanketed Europe hit Bergen, Norway. Spread by the fleas on rats, this plague caused ugly swellings, and its victims usually died within a few days of becoming infected. One-third of the entire population of Bergen was wiped out, and trade between the two countries stopped. This was catastrophic for the Vikings; the major Norwegian port had been Greenland's primary trading partner, and its king, who by then had a rich monopoly on trade with Greenland, refused to let any other country attempt trade with the Greenland Vikings. The last known trade ship from Bergen visited Greenland in 1367.

As Greenland's climate changed, the Thule Inuit ("too-lay in-you-it"), native Arctic peoples

2

John Davis Dances with Inuit and Explores the Davis Straits and Labrador, 1585–1587

Davis saw thousands of minke whales like this one.

The English explorer John Davis (~1550–1605) explored the Arctic at an exceptionally exciting time in European history. The so-called Dark Ages had already given way to the Renaissance, a period when arts and ideas flourished across Europe from the mid-1300s into the 1500s. After the Renaissance came the Age of Discovery, when European explorers mapped areas of the world from the Azores to the Americas. Davis lived during this period under the rule of Queen Elizabeth I, who reigned from 1558 to 1603—a very long time for one person to rule a country! Queen Elizabeth I was very much interested in exploring and claiming new lands. The Spanish and Portuguese were far ahead of England in the race for discoveries, and England badly wanted to catch up.

Under the queen's authority, Francis Drake circumnavigated (circled by ship) the entire globe, and Martin Frobisher explored Baffin Island west of Greenland. On the island, he found a dead narwhal (an arctic sea mammal whose males have a long, twisted ivory tusk), and delivered its tusk to the royal court, along with some ore that he thought was rich in gold (it was not). Frobisher had also brought several Inuit back to England as curiosities for the Queen and her court, all of whom became ill and died soon after arriving.

John Davis wanted to explore new lands as well, both for his own satisfaction and to win favor with the queen. As a boy, Davis had loved to sail boats—any boats. He was mesmerized by stories of voyages and adventure (one of his childhood friends was Walter Raleigh, a colorful explorer who would later be knighted by the queen and become Sir Walter Raleigh). By 1583 Davis felt that he was old enough and knowledgeable enough to set sail on his own adventure. His primary goal was to find the Northwest Passage, a sea route that was said to connect Europe and Asia, although no one had ever seen it. If it did exist, however, the person who found the passage would win great riches and attention, because England would be able to use it to increase its trade with Asia. Only one previous explorer, John Cabot, had officially sought the Northwest Passage. His first attempt, in 1497, was not successful, and his

Skua gulls may look friendly, but any explorer who came too close to one might be whacked over the head by a wing powerful enough to kill him.

second, in 1498, was even less so: he and his five ships never returned home.

Rumors of a Northwest Passage had persisted ever since Europeans had begun mapping the Arctic. There was much disagreement on where, exactly, this passage was. Whalers, who spent much of their time out on the water, thought that the larger expanses of Arctic waters might lead to the Pacific Ocean. In England, the route considered most likely was northwest (through what is now Canada), but some thought that the passage lay in the northeast (over what is now Russia). By focusing on exploring the northern regions of the world, the English faced less competition than they would

have in the warmer, more hospitable southern regions. The Spanish and Portuguese explorers, for example, went south, rounding the tip of Africa or South America to reach the Orient. The French had established a vigorous fur trade in areas that are now part of the northern United States and southern Canada. And anyone going over the land through the Middle East toward Asia had to pay money to Turkish merchants along the way as a bribe for passage across their lands.

In addition to finding the elusive Northwest Passage, John Davis had other goals. He wanted to skillfully map—for the first time—the coastlines of the lands he and his crew encountered. He wanted to invent a more precise navigational device to guide mapping and sailing. He also planned to write books about his voyages—and indeed, he wrote five during his career.

Davis raised the money to cover the cost of his voyage from three rich Englishmen, readied his two ships (the *Moonshine* and the *Sunneshine*), hired his crew, and readied to set sail. "North for China!" he and his crew cheered as they headed out to sea on June 7, 1585. (Of course, he was not actually traveling to China; the cheer was a common rallying cry of explorers at the time, regardless of where they were headed.)

Davis headed northwest from England. The farther he and his crew traveled, the colder it became, until Davis found himself in a maze of land, ice, and water. He had entered the Arctic

Arctic Natives

The Inuit, native peoples of the Arctic, inhabited the area thousands and thousands of years before the Europeans "discovered" it. The earliest groups arrived between 30,000 and 80,000 years ago, and by 5000 B.C., were well established across the Arctic. They are described as being *circumpolar* because groups of these natives live in all the lands circling the North Pole, from Russia to Alaska, Canada to Scandinavia.

Their livelihood in early days came from hunting whales, polar bears, seals, seabirds, and other sea creatures, following the caribou herd migrations across the tundra, and, later, herding reindeer (in Scandinavia). They built igloos and huts to live in. At one time all of the natives were called simply "Eskimos" by explorers, but the Inuit, the original settlers of the Arctic, are made up of several different groups, and today most people refer to them by their correct names: Thule Inuit, Yupik, Inupiat, and Inuvialuit, depending upon which area of the Arctic they inhabit.

Circle. The Arctic Circle is an area, designated on maps by a circle, that crosses Greenland, Norway's north islands, Russia, and Alaska. An immense and varied world of coldness located above 66 degrees 33 minutes north latitude, the Arctic Circle encompasses about 12 million square miles of land and water, including the Arctic Ocean, which covers about 5,600,000 square miles (not counting Hudson Bay).

Peering out at the icy waters that surrounded him and his nervous crew, Davis silently thanked his financial backers for having allowed him to bring a four-piece orchestra along on the journey. This is not as strange as it may seem. Arctic voyages were extremely dangerous, and sailors were known to *mutiny* (revolt against the captain). Encountering icebergs, sea ice, pack ice, pressure ridges, halo-like rings around the sun called sun dogs, and many more unfamiliar atmospheric and weather-related events, whole crews sometimes asked or even forced the captain to return home. Davis probably thought the band would boost morale of everyone onboard and help prevent a mutiny on his own ships.

The first land that Davis and his crew saw after entering the Arctic was the shoreline of eastern Greenland. Sea ice prevented them from landing there, so the two ships continued around the tip of Greenland, then north along its western coast. They landed, accompanied by the loud rush of tides, near the long-abandoned settlement of Erik the Red and the Vikings. Once on land, John Davis wrote the following words in his journal. (Note that he uses a "y" when we would normally use an "i," as well as some unusual words and punctuation, all of which were common at the time. "Conceites" means "weird or fanciful ideas.")

> The irksome noyse of the yse was such, that it bred strange conceites among us, so that we supposed the place to be vast and voyd of any sensible or vegitable creatures, whereupon I called the same Desolation.

Davis and his crew were on land for only a short while before they sighted native Inuit, who had launched their kayaks and were yelling at the English explorers. Assessing the situation, Davis quietly told the orchestra to play and ordered his men to dance around. The Inuit stopped in their tracks, amazed. They seem to have expected a fight, but Davis's quick thinking soothed the natives' fears. The Inuit quickly gave the strangers some gifts (most likely food, jewelry, or trinkets the Inuit were wearing or carrying), then left. The next morning the natives returned to the same spot, this time with drums. Dancing, they beckoned to the English explorers. Davis and his crew joined the natives, and together the two groups danced to the beat of the drums. They were unable to speak each other's language, but, through music and dancing, they communicated their friendliness and goodwill. This was a unique event in the history of exploration.

Continuing their journey, Davis's ships reached Baffin Island via a broad channel of water that lay between western Greenland and Baffin Island. (This channel was later named the Davis Straits, in honor of John Davis's expedition.) As the crew headed north into Baffin Bay and Cumberland Sound, a place crowded with whales at this time, Davis remained optimistic about finding the elusive Northwest Passage. But August had arrived, and it was time for the group to end its explorations and sail back to England in order to avoid the clutch of winter (which begins very early in the polar world). The small wooden ships could not last through the winter in the Arctic.

In 1586 Davis ventured out into the sea again in another attempt to find the passage. He was given even more money by benefactors to fund this trip than he'd had the first time, and he decided to take four, not two, ships on the journey. Heading north, Davis and his crew once again stopped on the Greenland coast, but this time they were greeted by a different group of natives who weren't as friendly as the ones they had danced with; some of them even threw rocks at the explorers. They also saw immense icebergs, which frightened them, but the gathering sea ice terrified some of the men even more than the icebergs. Davis saw their intense fear and knew that they might soon panic—or revolt against him. He gave those who were too terrified to continue permission to return home on one of the ships. Peace was maintained, and mutiny was avoided.

Make a Model Igloo

All over the Arctic, native people build igloos. Some igloos serve as temporary housing for hunting trips; other, larger ones are more permanent homes. There are two tricks to making a good igloo: creating the right kind of hole at the top and using snow as "glue" to hold the blocks of ice together.

A standard-sized igloo features 15 large blocks of ice or very dense snow, placed in a circle to form the base. The very top circle is created using about 5 blocks, placed in a circle with a hole in the center. Additional circles of ice blocks fill up the space between the base and the top of the igloo. The small hole at the top is covered with a bit of dried grass. The heat that is created by blubber-fueled lamps used in the igloo and by the inhabitants' body temperatures rises and escapes through the hole. (*Blubber* is the fat of whales, seals, or other large mammals.) Without that hole, the heat inside the igloo could melt its walls from the inside out. A small hall or passageway into the igloo keeps blasts of cold air from entering; it also functions as a double door and a storage area. Using excel-

Materials
Adult supervision required
Several trays of ice cubes
One or more very sharp knives
Boiling water
Cookie sheet or other flat tray that is at least
10 inches by 10 inches and that fits in your freezer
Teaspoon
Bowl of snow (kept in the freezer until used), jar of marshmallow sauce, or container of white frosting

lent ice knives, a skilled Inuit can build an igloo like this for a family in about an hour.

1. Remove 12 cubes from the freezer and place them in a circle on the cookie sheet. Place the cookie sheet in the freezer and let the ice cubes on it freeze solid again. (Do this each time you add a layer to your igloo.) While these are freezing, you can go on to step 2.

2. Prepare the ice cubes that will be used for the second layer. Remove one ice cube from the freezer. Dip the sharp knife into the boiling water until it's hot, then cut off one-fourth of the ice cube, so that the cube is narrower than, but just as long as, the ones that form the base. (Note: If you have difficulty cutting the ice cube, try using a different sharp knife. Some will work

5. Remove the ice cube halves and the cookie sheet from the freezer. Place the cut cubes on top of the ones on the cookie sheet, lining them up so that each cut cube is centered over the ends of two cubes and is flush with the inside of the cubes under it. Fill the spaces between the cubes with snow, marshmallow sauce, or frosting, and place the cookie sheet back into the freezer.

6. Continue cutting smaller and smaller pieces of ice, placing them on top of the cubes on the cookie sheet as you did in the previous steps until you have just a small hole in the center of the top. (Don't forget to refreeze your creation once in a while as you work.)

7. Choose where you'd like the door to your igloo to be. Using snow, marshmallow sauce, or frosting, make the outline of a low-arched door, starting at the bottom of the base and going up about one-fourth of the way to the top. (The doorway to a real igloo is cut out, of course, but this is just a model.) Refreeze.

8. Build a hall leading up to the door. Line up two rows of ice cubes lengthwise, starting from the doorway and going straight out, to make the walls of your hall. There should be about a half-inch or so of space between your walls. Place ice cubes on top of the walls to make a roof for the hall. Fill in the gaps between the ice cubes with snow, marshmallow sauce, or frosting. Pat a thin layer of snow, or spread a thin layer of marshmallow sauce or frosting, over the entire igloo.

9. Place the igloo in the freezer for at least a couple of hours. When it is frozen solid, you can display it to your friends and family!

better than others, although it's unlikely that any will work as well as the special tools the Inuit use.) Place the cut cube back in the freezer, remove another ice cube, and repeat the process until you have cut 10 cubes like this.

3. Remove the cut ice cubes and the cookie sheet with the circle of cubes from the freezer. Place the cut cubes on top of the ones on the cookie sheet. Line them up so that each cut cube is centered over the ends of two base cubes and is flush with the inside of the base cubes. As you add layers, you'll see that each ring is smaller than

the one under it, creating a dome. Using the teaspoon, carefully fill in the cracks between the cubes with damp snow or a very thin layer of marshmallow sauce or frosting to help keep them in place. Place the cookie sheet back into the freezer and let the ice cubes freeze solid. You can complete step 4 while these ice cubes are refreezing.

4. Remove one ice cube from the freezer. Dip your sharp knife into the boiling water to heat it, and cut the cube in half lengthwise. Place the halves in the freezer, remove another ice cube, and repeat the process. Do this until you have eight halves.

Sea ice could trap a ship and its crew for months at a time.

What About Longitude?

Early explorers also wanted to travel farther west than anyone had previously done, but this did not earn them as much acclaim and fanfare as traveling north did. The reason is that, at the time, there was no way to accurately measure *longitude*, the method of determining location and measuring distance by using imaginary fixed horizontal lines to encircle Earth. On seafaring voyages, longitude is measured by a ship's clock, and it would be many years after Davis's explorations before a clock that would accurately measure longitude would be invented.

Icebergs are dangerous for explorers because they can break apart suddenly. The base of the iceberg, hidden under water, is sometimes much wider than its visible top; it can tear apart any ship that comes too close to it.

Once again winter approached, and Davis was forced to end his search for the Northwest Passage and return to England. On the way back, he explored and mapped Labrador. There he encountered natives who were very hostile. They killed two of his crewmen and wounded three more. Even worse, while they were traveling around Labrador a fierce storm sank one of the three remaining ships. Davis and his remaining crew were relieved to reach England before more calamity—or the Arctic winter—descended upon them.

Davis made a third attempt to find the Northwest Passage in 1587, this time with three ships. Like his previous voyage, this journey was not problem-free. The native people that he and his crew encountered were again unwelcoming. One of the ships sprung a bad

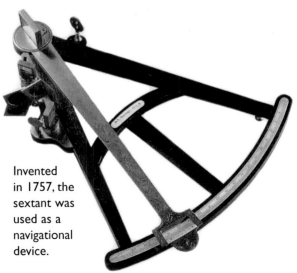

Invented in 1757, the sextant was used as a navigational device.

Orcas

Once called killer whales, these majestic black-and-white mammals were made famous in the movie *Free Willy*. They are dramatic sea predators, and they were observed by all the Arctic explorers.

Slicing the water like a thick torpedo, the orca's body is a study in power and speed. This animal commands respect and fear in every ocean of the world. Even the immense blue whale is powerless to defend itself against an attack by a pod (group) of orcas. To seals, sea lions, dolphins, and other small marine mammals, the appearance of an orca means sudden death. The whalers and sailors who dubbed these creatures "wolves of the sea" had good reason to do so.

With their six-foot-high dorsal fins and distinctive markings, orcas are unmistakable. Black dorsally (in back) and white ventrally (in front), they are further marked by an oval spot behind each eye. Just behind the dorsal fin of many orcas lies a gray patch called a saddle (because it is shaped like a horse saddle). Not all orcas have a saddle, and the patch varies in size and shape, making it a helpful marker in identifying individual whales. Orcas have 10 to 13 pairs of interlocking conical teeth in both their upper and lower jaws. As the largest member of the dolphin family, orcas reach lengths of up to 30 feet, with males a little bigger than females. The largest known orca weighed in at about nine tons.

leak, and, to avoid a mutiny, Davis had to send more crew members home to England. Eventually Davis and his remaining crew were forced to turn back to avoid another Arctic winter. Although he did travel farther up the Greenland coast than he ever had before, John Davis never found the passage that had captured his imagination.

Davis's explorations were successful in many other ways, however. During his three Arctic voyages, he mapped most of the Labrador coast, hundreds of miles of western Greenland, and parts of Baffin Island. He wrote the first descriptions of the area's wildlife, native peoples, currents, and ice conditions. And he had wanted to travel as far north—to get as close to the North Pole—as he possibly could. According to the rules of latitude, the equator is at zero latitude and the geographic North Pole is at 90 degrees north latitude. The closer a ship came to 90 degrees north latitude, the closer it was to the top of the world. While he did not make it all the way to the North Pole, John Davis ventured as far as 72 degrees 12 minutes north latitude, farther than anyone had gone before.

At least, that's what Europeans told themselves. In reality, native peoples of these regions, as well as the Greenland Vikings, had surely ventured farther north than did any of the European explorers of the Age of Discovery. Somehow, however, this fact didn't count for much in the 16th-century European worldview (just as it didn't seem to count that native peoples had been living on this "new land" for thousands and thousands of years before the Europeans "discovered" it).

John Davis is also credited with developing a *ship's log* (a navigation diary) and inventing a directional device called a *backstaff* (a navigational device that measured the altitude of the sun), both of which influenced exploration for nearly 100 years. His ship's log was the first of any explorer's to record all the ice conditions, wildlife, weather, and native peoples he encountered. Despite his failure to find the Northwest Passage, Davis's voyages were considered great successes.

In the last years of his life, Davis explored the Falkland Islands (near Antarctica), and in 1587 he made one last attempt to find the Northwest Passage, this time journeying over the Pacific Ocean. He made it only as far as Singapore, where he was killed by pirates.

Make a Cross-Staff to Measure Latitude

The cross-staff, also called the *English quadrant*, is one of the earliest instruments devised to measure a ship's latitude. It's used at night. In contrast, a backstaff is used during daylight.

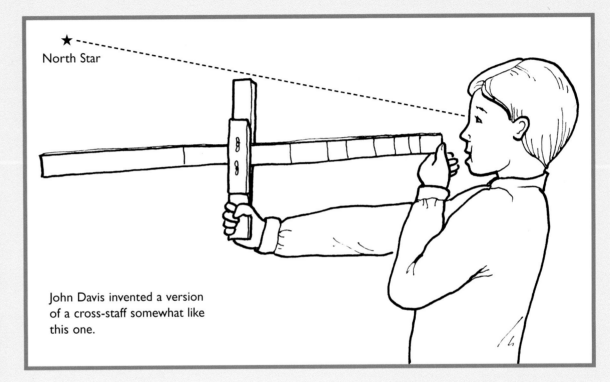

John Davis invented a version of a cross-staff somewhat like this one.

Materials

Adult supervision required	2 2½-inch-long carriage bolts
Ruler	2 wing nuts for carriage bolts
Pen	Protractor
1 5-inch-long, 2-inch-wide, 1-inch-thick piece of wood	Yardstick
1 12-inch-long, 2-inch-wide, 1-inch-thick piece of wood	Piece of sandpaper (fine or medium grade)
1 3-foot-long, 1½-inch-wide, 1-inch-thick piece of wood	11 small containers of acrylic paint (each a different color)
Electric drill	Small paintbrush
Drill bit that is slightly larger than the bolts (see next item)	Black marker
	Dark night

1. Using the ruler and the pen, find and mark the center of the length of the 5-inch-long piece of wood.
2. Measure and draw two lines across the 5-inch piece of wood: one ¾ of an inch to the right of the center mark, and the other ¾ of an inch to the left of the center mark.
3. Make two large dots; each one centered and just outside the two lines.
4. Ask an adult to drill holes through the 5-inch piece where you have made the two dots.
5. Place the 5-inch piece of wood in the center of the 12-inch piece of wood (parallel to the 12-inch piece, so that one is stacked on top of the other). Poke the pen into each of the holes, marking the 12-inch piece of wood.
6. Ask an adult to drill holes through the 12-inch piece where you have made the two marks.

7. Place the 5-inch-long piece onto the 12-inch-long piece so that the holes line up. Put the bolts in through the two sets of holes. Attach the wing nuts and tighten just enough to keep the wing nuts from falling off.

8. Gently slide the 3-foot-long piece into the space between the bolts so that it is between and perpendicular to the two other pieces of wood. Carefully slide the two bolted pieces down so that they are about 4 inches from one end of the 3-foot piece. Check the wing nuts to make sure they are still secure.

9. Place the protractor on the other end of the 3-foot piece so that the center point of its flat side is just at the wood's edge, and the curved part of the protractor is above the wood and perpendicular to it.

10. Stand the device on its end so that the protractor is at the top and the 3-foot-long piece of wood is parallel to the floor. Take the yardstick and place it with one end balanced at the end of the longest piece in front of the protractor, and the other end balanced on top of the whole three-piece device.

11. Slide the smaller pieces and the yardstick enough so that the yardstick is lined up with the 10-degree line on the protractor.

12. With the pen, draw a line across the flat part of the long stick to mark that position (on the left side of the vertical part of the device).

13. Slide the device to the 15-degree position and mark that position.

14. Do the same every 5 degrees, up to 65 or 70 degrees.

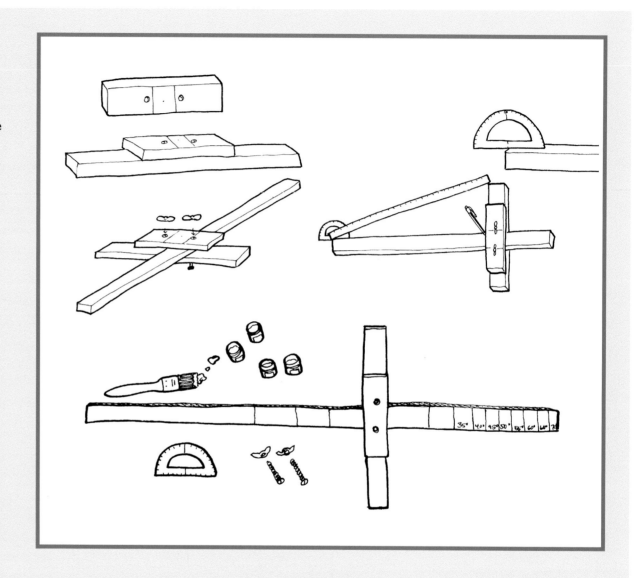

15. Disassemble the cross-staff and paint each marked-off area in a different color. Paint the two shorter pieces each in two different colors from each other (but they can be the same as any of the sections of the longer piece).

16. Using the marker, relabel the numbers so that they are easier to read.

17. After everything is dry, put the device back together.

18. On a dark night, find the North Star in the sky. It is the medium-bright star that is lined up with the two stars in the Big Dipper that form the side of the Dipper farthest from the handle—when you find these two stars, look up higher in the sky from them in an imaginary line until you see it. The North Star is also called Polaris.

19. Loosen the wing nuts on your cross-staff enough so that you can slide the long piece. Hold the long side parallel to the ground and at eye level, with the higher numbers closer to your face than the lower ones.

20. Line up the device pointing at the North Star, keeping the long stick parallel to the ground. Slide the crosspiece so that the top tip is just below the North Star. Hold it in place there, tightening the wing nuts a bit if necessary.

21. Find the number closest to where the crosspiece crosses the long wood piece. This is your latitude!

22. You can do this anywhere in the Northern Hemisphere to find your latitude.

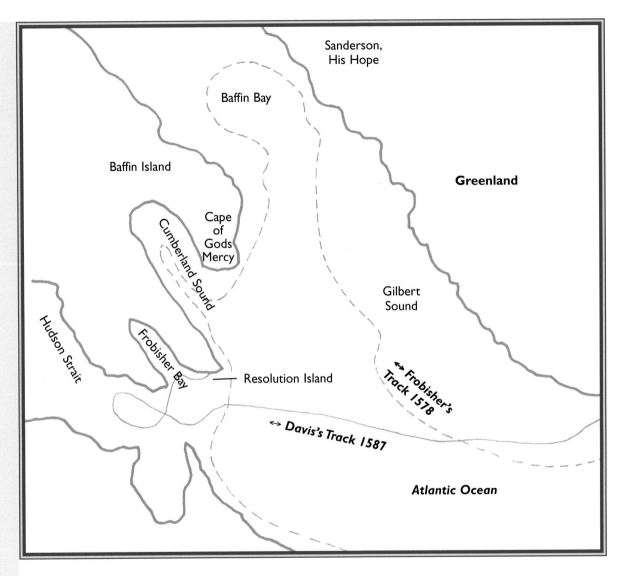

This map shows Davis's route in 1587, along with a route previously taken by explorer Martin Frobisher.

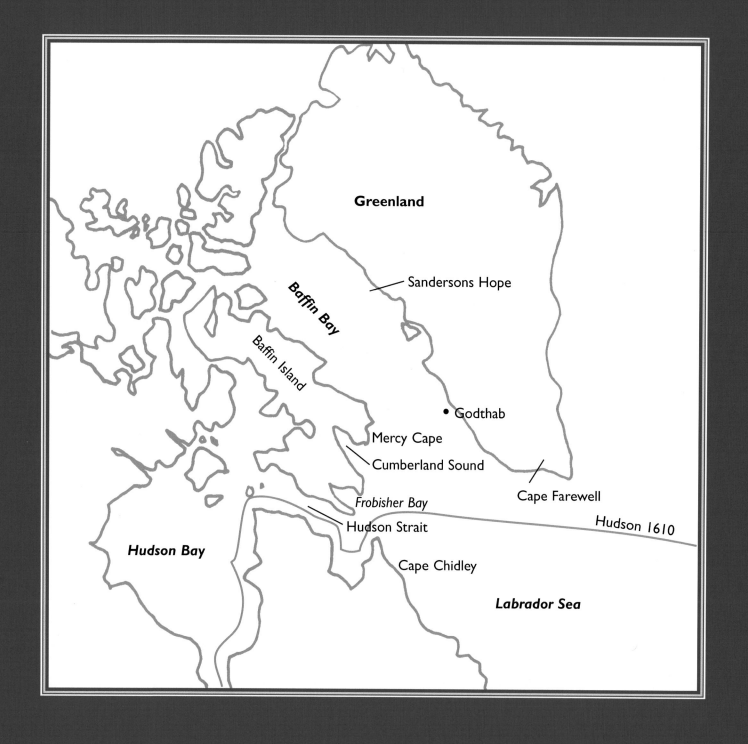

Greenland

Sandersons Hope

Baffin Bay

Baffin Island

• Godthab

Mercy Cape

Cumberland Sound

Cape Farewell

Frobisher Bay

Hudson Strait

Hudson 1610

Hudson Bay

Cape Chidley

Labrador Sea

3

Henry Hudson Ventures Northwest and Northeast in Search of a Passage, 1607–1610

John Davis's failure to find the legendary Northwest Passage didn't stop people from believing that such a route from Europe to the Orient did exist, and finding it remained the "golden goal" of explorers. William Barents, a Dutch explorer, made three attempts (in 1594, 1595, and 1596) to locate a passage. On his third attempt in 1596, his ship became trapped by sea ice. Barents and his crew made it to the shore of Novaya Zemlya, located northeast of the Kola Peninsula of Russia, and were forced to stay there the entire winter. Barely sheltered by the cabin they cobbled together from driftwood, they battled starvation, disease, bear attacks, and the brutal cold. Barents and his crew became the first West Europeans to winter in the high Arctic and survive. In June 1597 they

Hudson took this route in his exploration of the bay that now bears his name.

set out on a 1,600-mile escape in two open boats. Barents died during the journey, but many of his men survived, and they returned with the insightful weather records that Barents had collected during their winter in the Arctic. These records would later prove useful to Henry Hudson and other explorers who would make their own Arctic journeys.

Gerrit de Veer, a crewmember who made it safely back to Europe, published a popular account of their venture. The book's title says it all—and then some:

The True and Perfect Description of Three Voyages, so strange and wonderfull, that the like hath neuer been heard of before: Done and performed three yeares, one after the other, by ships of Holland and Zeeland, on the North sides of Norway, Muscouia, and Tartaria, toward the Kingdomes of Cathia and China; shewing the discouerie of the Straightes of Weigates, Noua Zembla, and the countrie lying under 80 degrees; which is thought to be Greenland: where neuer any man had bin before: with the cruell Beares, and other Monsters of the Sea, and the unsupportable and extreame cold that is found in those places. And how in that last Voyage, the Shippe was so inclosed by the ice, that it was left there, whereby the men were forced to build a house in the cold and desart Countrie of Noua Zembla, wherein they continued 10 monthes together, and neuer saw nor heard of any man in, most great cold and extreame miserie; and how after that, to saue their lives, they were constrained to sayle aboue 350 Dutch miles, which is aboue 1000 English, in little open Boates, along and ouer the Maine Seas, in most great danger, and with extreame labour, unspeakable troubles, and great hunger.

A few other, more minor, attempts to find a passage were made by Dutch and British explorers, all without success. Englishman Henry Hudson decided to give it a try.

Hudson (~1565–1611), an experienced seaman, set his sails north on four different voyages, each time under the hire of companies (three English and one Dutch) who wanted to find a route to the Orient in order to increase their trade. On his first Arctic venture in 1607 he took along 10 crewmen and his son John, who was about 10 years old at the time.

Unlike other explorers who looked for a passage in the northwest, Hudson searched for a Northeast Passage. (Nobody had proof that *any* passage existed, but some explorers, such as Hudson, thought that a Northeast Passage was more likely to exist, or that it would be easier to find.) He and his crew traveled along Greenland's east coast, a route that was considered the most promising by the English at the time. Along the way they made detailed maps of the coastline. They continued to head north until they encountered huge amounts of sea ice that blocked them from

Seabirds like these fish for their food all over the Arctic.

going farther north. Changing direction, they sailed east toward Spitsbergen, an Arctic island north of Norway. Today Spitsbergen is a favorite destination of tourists who want to see the polar bears that inhabit the land, but at the time that Hudson traveled there it was home only to thousands of whales. Hudson reached 80 degrees 23 minutes north latitude, the farthest north that any European explorer had traveled, before having to end his journey and head back to England in order to avoid the Arctic winter. Because of his explorations in this area, a vigorous whaling industry was soon established near Spitsbergen.

The next year, in 1608, the same English company (the wealthy Muscovy Company)

Polar Bears

The largest of all land carnivores, polar bears are common throughout the Arctic. (They do not live in Antarctica at all.) Virtually every North Pole explorer sees them, and as John Davis wrote, ". . . when wee came neere the shore, wee found them to be white beares of a monstruous bignesse. . . ." The Inuit word for this animal means "he who is without shadow."

These bears hunt with stealth and are superbly camouflaged—they even hold up one of their white paws to cover their black noses as they stalk their prey on the ice. Standing as tall as 10 feet and weighing 1,000–1,600 pounds when fully grown, they are strong enough to swoop up a 500-pound seal with one paw. Polar bears can run as fast as 25 miles per hour. They're good swimmers, too, and they can dive under the water to catch sea birds. Polar bears have excellent eyesight, even at night, and they can smell a living meal (such as a seal) from 20 miles away.

---

hired him to venture in search of the elusive Northeast Passage again. This time Hudson aimed more directly northeast, nearing Spitsbergen again and rounding Norway's North Cape. He got as far east as the Barents Sea

before the season began to change. Winter was coming, so Hudson and his crew turned back and headed for home. All in all, it was a fairly uneventful trip, although at one point the crew spotted something mysterious in the ocean—it was a mermaid! At least, this is what they believed, and Hudson dutifully noted their observation in his ship's log.

In 1609 Hudson was hired once again, this time by the Dutch East India Trading Company (one of the first multinational corporations in the world, it organized trade among countries in Europe). He was provided a ship—the *Half Moon Bay*—and a crew of 10 Englishmen and 10 Dutchmen. The company instructed Hudson to head northeast again in search of a Northeast Passage. Hudson was also told to return to port if he encountered difficult weather conditions. Many people, including Hudson's employers, were beginning to doubt the existence of a passage; while the company was optimistic enough to pay for another attempt to find it, the owners hoped to keep costs at a minimum. They certainly did not want to lose a ship, or to pay Hudson to spend a winter stuck in the Arctic.

Hudson disobeyed his instructions to head northeast. Instead, he decided to look for a Northwest Passage, and he sailed far west in search of it, eventually reaching North America. In what is now New York State, he sailed up the Hudson River for about 150 miles, to what is now Albany. He hoped that he had finally found the elusive Northwest Passage, but the crew was

Food, Glorious Food

Sailors on a European Arctic voyage of this era typically lived on salt beef, smoked cod (a kind of fish), dried peas, cheese, bread and butter, and beer, all of which were brought along for the journey. Along the way, they also fished for fresh cod, and they hunted and ate animals such as seals and polar bears. Food was always a concern, however; if a ship ran out of provisions, its captain could expect a mutiny sometime soon.

---

restless; one, Robert Juet, almost succeeded in engineering a mutiny. Hudson concluded that this river was not the Northwest Passage and agreed to return east and south. As they did, they stopped at the island that is now called Manhattan. Hudson claimed the land for the Dutch. The English government was distinctly annoyed that he had done this (he may have been working for a Dutch company, but he was still an Englishman, after all). Upon his return to England, his sponsors forbade him from sailing under any foreign flags in the future.

Hudson's last voyage, and his most elaborate, was paid for by 18 wealthy individuals, the Mus-

A Puzzle and a Theory About January Temperatures

Hudson and his crew experienced the vast emptiness of the Arctic on their journeys.

covy Company, and the Dutch East India Company. Hudson and his men were set to *overwinter* (to stay throughout the winter) in the Arctic on their ship, the *Discovery*. Hudson set sail on April 17, 1610, with his son John and a crew that once again included Robert Juet. (Although he had almost started a mutiny during Hudson's previous voyage, Juet's skills made him a valuable crewman.)

Sailing northwest from Europe, the *Discovery* became icebound near Hudson Bay. Juet

As Henry Hudson and his crew explored the Arctic both to the northwest and to the northeast, they encountered a range of temperatures, even during the summer. Why would this be? It's a phenomenon that occurs in all four seasons, but the puzzle is probably easiest to figure out when we use a range of winter temperatures to solve it.

> **Materials**
> Pencil
> Sticky notes
> Globe
> Atlas with
>   individually
>   detailed maps of
>
> Alaska, Greenland,
> Sweden, Finland,
> Russia, Mongolia,
> and China
> Paper

1. Write the name of each northern city listed below and its average January temperature on a Post-it note (one location per note).

Anchorage, Alaska	12° F (–11 °C)
Fairbanks, Alaska	–12° F (–24 °C)
Godthåb, Greenland	18° F (–8 °C)
Haparando, Sweden	12° F (–11 °C)
Harbin, China	–1° F (–18 °C)
Kuopio, Finland	14° F (–10 °C)
Saratov, Russia	11° F (–12 °C)
Sverdlovsk, Russia	9° F (–13 °C)
Thule, Greenland	–12° F (–24 °C)
Tihua, China	–3° F (–19 °C)
Tomsk, Russia	–6° F (–21 °C)
Ulaanbaatar, Mongolia	–14° F (–26 °C)

2. Find and mark, with the pencil or the corner of a sticky note, each city on both the globe and the atlas.
3. Place each sticky note back onto the globe in the proper place.
4. Now it's time to develop your theory: Why this temperature pattern? Hint: It is not true that the temperatures simply get colder as you move north. The answer is in the Selected Answers chapter in the back of the book.
5. Think about how life in each of these countries might differ for its inhabitants in terms of diet, clothing, shelter, and other essentials depending on the weather.

demanded that Hudson change the ship's route. Hudson, again fearing mutiny, complied. The *Discovery* headed south along the Bay's east coast, where Hudson explored James Bay. Winter arrived, and throughout the long, cold season, the crew became more and more restless. They accused each other of taking more than their fair share of the food. They also accused Hudson of providing more food to favored crewmembers. By June, which is usually Spring in the area, the men were in turmoil.

Mutiny! On June 22, 1611, Juet and another crew member commandeered the ship. They forced Hudson, his son John, and several others into a small boat and set them adrift in the ocean, toward almost certain death. The remaining crew then headed back for England. On the way, Juet and some of the other crewmen were killed by Inuit, but the *Discovery* did eventually make it home.

Hudson, his son, and the others who had been abandoned were never seen again.

Blowing Soap Bubbles into the Cold

Explorers such as Henry Hudson noticed that unexpected things often happened to common materials and items in the very cold Arctic climate (like shoe leather suddenly splitting for no apparent reason). If you live in a place with very low temperatures or have a freezer, you can see that even bubbles sometimes act very strangely!

Materials

Bubble-blowing solution and wand	Very cold air (below 0° F, or −18° C)

---

1. Blow bubbles, one by one, into the coldest air you can find. Doing this outside on a day when the temperature is below zero (especially way below!) is best—but using an indoor freezer works, too.
2. Observe how the bubbles look and act when blown into very cold air. You'll see that, unlike bubbles blown outside on a warm summer day, these will not stay round, and it won't take an object such as a bush or your finger to pop them, either. Instead, they may shatter like glass while still in midair. They may deflate and twist into a piece of rubberlike skin. They may take on very strange shapes. The colder the air, the more dramatic the bubbles' looks and actions will be. The most dramatic changes occur in extremely cold air (−20° F, or −29° C, and colder).

Why does this happen? A bubble is made of a little bit of soap, a lot of water, and your warm breath. When a bubble is blown in very cold air, its water quickly freezes into tiny ice crystals. These ice crystals are so small that you can't see them. But they are big enough to partly break or even shatter the bubble. At the same time, the warm air inside the bubble expands, as all warm air does. This creates more pressure on the bubble. The very cold air quickly stops that expansion, however, and often causes the bubble to shatter, or to take on some strange shape before it deflates. This helps to break the bubble, too.

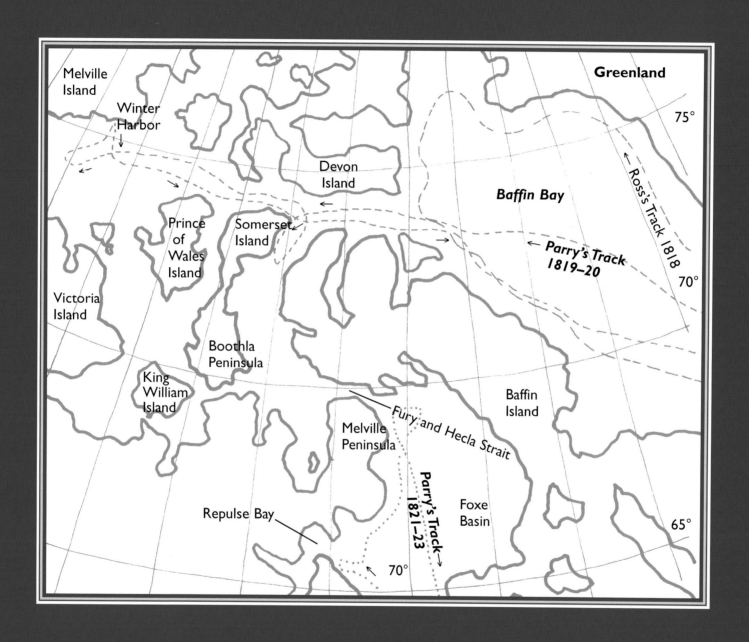

4

William Parry Explores Lancaster Sound and Beyond, 1819–1820, 1821–1823, 1824–1825, and 1827

After Henry Hudson's death in 1611, the push to find a passage to the Orient and to reach the North Pole diminished. During the next 200 years, few people explored the Arctic. Instead, people set up commercial enterprises there, in order to make money from the natural resources that had been discovered. One of the biggest enterprises there at the time was *whaling* (killing whales and selling their meat, blubber, and other body parts).

The whaling industry, which flourished for 300 years after Henry Hudson's death, was especially vigorous and intense around Spitsbergen (north of mainland Norway). There, huge numbers of finbacks, humpbacks, blue whales, and sperm whales were harpooned (killed with a *harpoon*, a long, barbed spear). Information

The routes of two of William Parry's Arctic voyages.

The White Wolf of the Arctic

Most people are familiar with the timber wolf, the gray wolf, and possibly the red wolf (which has been reintroduced into the Carolinas), but very few know of the existence of the white wolf. William Parry saw these magnificent animals, and he wrote about them in his journal:

> A wolf, which crossed the harbour close to the ships on the 25th, was observed to be almost entirely white, his body long and extremely lean, standing higher on his legs than any of the Esquimaux dogs, but otherwise much resembling them; his tail was long and bushy, and always hanging between his legs, and he kept his head very low in running. It is extraordinary that we could never succeed in killing or catching one of these animals, though we were, for months, almost constantly endeavouring to do so.

White wolves howl, raise their pups together, and otherwise behave like any other kind of wolf. Their distinct feature is their fur, which is an excel-lent camouflage in their Arctic environment. Pure white, these beautiful animals almost look as though they've been dipped in snow. This helps them catch and kill their prey: small rodents of the Arctic tundra and the giant musk oxen who also live there.

Scientists have watched these wolves coordinate their stalking of musk oxen, which are about the size of buffaloes. When under attack, groups of musk oxen form a circle, facing their horned heads and strong hoofs outward in order to defend themselves, and keeping the baby musk oxen inside the circle. Musk oxen are not easy prey. The wolves' best strategy is to try to kill a baby before the circle forms, and they do not succeed at this often.

Once thought to be a myth, the white wolf was not seen by modern scientists until about 25 years ago, and although the wolves have been studied for the last quarter-century, much about them remains to be learned. These days, scientists are focusing their studies on the white wolves of Ellesmere Island (west of northern Greenland), particularly a pack that lives in a wolf den under a rocky overhang. These wolves have very little fear of people, so scientists are keeping their location a secret to protect them from humans who might harm them.

Sir William Parry was made a knight because of his successful explorations.

on whaling grounds (locations where one could find many whales) was very valuable, and most whalers wanted to keep their own maps of whaling grounds secret and out of the hands of competitors. William Scoresby, a scientist and an explorer as well as a whaler, was an exception to this rule. He reached 81 degrees 21 minutes north latitude in 1806, and his studies of whales and

Parry and his men saw dramatic icescapes while at sea.

whaling grounds, which he wrote about in books, provided much information that had never before been documented. Scoresby's son, William Scoresby, Jr., followed in his father's footsteps, and also made significant scientific advances and documented his findings about the Arctic.

Whaling was not the only industry in the Arctic. The fur trade, in which people killed animals and sold their fur, was also booming, especially in what is now Canada and the northern United States. Here, the Hudson Bay Company bought thousands and thousands of furs, both from Europeans who were doing business there and from the area natives, then sold them in Europe.

General exploration of the Arctic did not completely end, however. Peter the Great of Russia ordered an expedition into Arctic Siberia in the early 1700s. The Russians also explored the Bering Straits and came very close to North America, but it was so foggy that they never saw it! More Russian explorers mapped the Bering Straits between 1733 and 1745. One expedition included a scientist, who recorded details of the Arctic and subarctic wildlife.

Why did England temporarily lose interest in exploring the Arctic? One reason was war. The British endured a civil war in the 1600s, naval wars with France and Spain, and the American Revolutionary War. That's enough to distract anybody from exploration! After the War of 1812, however, John Barrow, a naval officer who worked at the powerful government agency called the British Admiralty (similar to the U.S. Navy), decided it was time to revive the search for a passage to the Orient and the quest to reach the North Pole. He believed that once ships passed what is now Baffin Island (west of Greenland), they could sail relatively easily, through open water, directly into the Pacific Ocean.

Barrow commissioned two simultaneous voyages for the British government, each with multiple ships, in 1818. One was led by John Ross, and it included Lieutenant William Parry,

This painting shows Sir John Ross exploring Baffin Bay.

who was second in command. (The other was led by David Buchan, and included John Franklin, the subject of the next chapter, as second in command.) One group sailed northeast via Spitsbergen; the other, northwest via Baffin Bay. They planned to meet in the Bering Strait after discovering the passage. Although this did not happen, both Parry and Franklin received valuable Arctic training on these voyages.

In 1819, William Parry (1790–1855), then 29 years of age, was given command of two ships—the *Hecla* and the *Griper*—and commissioned by the British Admiralty to seek the Northwest Passage. A prize was also announced: the first explorer to discover the Northwest Passage would receive an extra 5,000 British pounds. This was a tremendous amount of money at the time. Parry was ready to win that bonus prize!

On this Arctic voyage Parry explored Lancaster Sound to Melville Island, mapping a great deal of what would later be named the Parry Channel. He also discovered and named some nearby islands, including Somerset Island, Prince of Wales Island, and Devon Island, where the Parry expedition first heard the song of beluga whales (the white whales of the Arctic). At the time, Devon Island was very near the Magnetic North Pole's location. As they approached the Magnetic North Pole, Parry and his crew saw their compass needle wobble in a very weird way. Here is what Parry wrote in his report of that day in September 1819:

At a quarter-past nine P.M., we had the satisfaction of crossing the meridian of 110 degrees west from Greenwich, in the latitude of 74 degrees 44 minutes 20 seconds: by which His Majesty's ships, under my orders, became entitled to the sum of five thousand pounds, being the reward offered by the King's order in council, grounded on a late Act of Parliament, to such of His Majesty's subjects as might succeed in penetrating thus far to the westward within the Arctic Circle. In order to commemorate the success which had hitherto attended our exertions, the bluff head-land, which we had just passed, was subsequently called by the men BOUNTY CAPE; by which name I have, therefore, distinguished it on the chart ... and it created in us no ordinary feelings of pleasure to see the British flag waving, for the first time, in these

How Many Poles?

Unbelievable as it sounds, there is actually more than one North Pole. The Geographic North Pole, which is located at 90 degrees zero minutes north latitude, is what most people mean when they talk about the North Pole. It's also known as "true north," because it's as far north as you can get: walk in any direction from the North Pole, and you'll be walking south. The Geographic North Pole is a fixed place—it doesn't move around.

There is another North Pole, however, that is quite different from its geographic brother: the Magnetic North Pole. This is the spot that a magnetic compass points toward. Why does it exist, and why isn't it in the same place as the Geographic North Pole?

Like other planets, the Earth has a magnetic field. The Magnetic North Pole is the focus of this magnetic field in the north, and it's what a magnetic compass points toward. (As a compass gets close to it, however, its needle wobbles so much in reaction to the magnetic force that it's useless as a navigational tool.) Unlike the Geographic North Pole, the Magnetic North Pole does not stay in the same place all the time. The Earth's magnetic field is constantly shifting, which causes the location of the Magnetic North Pole to shift, too—on average, between 6 and 25 miles each year. Since its discovery in 1831, it has moved hundreds of miles. Currently the Magnetic North Pole lies about 1,000 miles south of the Geographic North Pole.

regions, which had hitherto been considered beyond the limits of the habitable part of the world. . . . After divine service had been performed, I assembled the officers, seamen, and marines of the *Hecla*, and announced to them officially, that their exertions had so far been crowned with success, as to entitle them to the first prize in the scale of rewards, granted by His Majesty's Order in Council

above mentioned ... I also addressed a letter to Lieutenant Liddon, to the same effect, and directed a small addition to be made to the usual allowance of meat, and some beer to be served, as a Sunday's dinner, on this occasion.

Parry did not realize that the location he and his party had reached was not the Geographic North Pole, but the Magnetic North Pole. His mistake was understandable. At the time, no one knew that a Magnetic North Pole existed at all; they simply relied on their compasses to tell them when they "reached true north."

In addition to finding the North Pole, Parry wanted to learn more about polar water currents and winds. Almost every day of his voyage he threw into the sea a bottle with a note inside that gave his ship's location. In the note, Parry asked the person who found the bottle to write down the latitude and longitude at which the message was found and to send this information to the British government. This would allow Parry later to study how the water currents and wind had pushed along a bottle to its final destination. He wrote each note in several languages; after all, who knew where the bottle would end up?

Parry tried to keep his crew busy and entertained during their long voyage. They grew watercress and mustard greens on the ship's deck during the spring and summer, and inside during the winter. During their first Arctic winter (late 1819 into 1820), the men performed popular comedy plays for each other, sang hymns, wrote and published their own newspaper, and attended daily exercise and other classes. They even tamed an Arctic fox to eat out of their hands. On this trip they saw their first walrus, which they called a horse whale. They also killed and studied a few polar bears before cooking their meat.

Make Polar Provisions

Polar explorers melted snow and ice to get plenty of water, and they shot birds, seals, walruses, and even polar bears for meat along the way. But they brought along a lot of food, too. They usually packed hardtack (a kind of hard bread made of flour and water) because it didn't rot. They also packed some fruits and vegetables, which they needed to avoid *scurvy*, a disease caused by not getting enough vitamin C. To keep them from rotting or being affected by the cold, the fruits and vegetables were canned or dried before the expedition.

You can experiment with drying your own foods in this activity.

Materials	
Adult supervision required	canned and drained)
2 apples	Freezer-safe tray
2 oranges	Knife
2 tomatoes	2 cookie sheets
1/2 cup cooked corn kernels (fresh or	Glass

1. Even if a piece of fruit was still fresh, how would it taste after being in the polar cold? To test this, put one apple, one orange, one tomato, and a few corn kernels on a freezer-safe tray. Place the tray in the freezer before you go to bed at night.
2. The next morning, take the tray out of the freezer. Warm the food by holding it between your hands just until it's thawed enough to slice or bite into. Eat a bite of each fruit and vegetable. Yuck! Most fruits and vegetables get mushy and taste bad when kept in very cold places such as a freezer—or the North Pole. The mushiness happens because fruits and vegetables contain a lot of water. The water expands and forms into little ice crystals as it freezes, turning the food into mush. Not only does this make the food taste bad, but it makes uneaten food rot very quickly. Which of these foods tastes the worst to you? Which tastes "just OK?" The corn probably tastes the best of all of these. That's because it has less water in it than the tomato, the apple, or the orange.
3. Now take a fresh apple, orange, and tomato and cut them into the thinnest slices you can make. Place the slices in a single layer on a dry cookie

sheet. Put the rest of the corn kernels on another cookie sheet. Using the glass, press down on them to flatten them out as much as possible. Spread the corn in a thin layer on the cookie sheet.

4. Place the cookie sheets in the oven. Heat the oven to the lowest temperature you can. (You want the warm air in the oven to dry out the food, not to cook it.) Keep the food in the oven until it is completely dried. (Check it after an hour or so, and then every half hour. The thinner the slices, the faster the food will dry.) When the food is dried, remove the cookie sheets from the oven.

5. Carefully place the slices in a single layer on a clean paper towel. Put another paper towel over them and gently press down to check for moisture. Place any of the fruits or vegetables that do not feel dry back onto a cookie sheet and into the oven. The goal is to get them very dry! When you can't feel any moisture in the food any more, turn off the oven and put the food on a plate or paper towel to cool.

6. Taste your dried food. Although most of the water has been taken out, they still taste pretty good, don't they? Place the dried food in the freezer for a couple of hours, and then taste it again. Not bad, eh? Very cold temperatures don't really affect the taste of dried foods very much, and the cold helps to keep mold from forming on the dried food as well.

7. Share your polar provisions with some friends and see how they like them.

After reaching the Magnetic North Pole, Parry sailed west for a while (as far as 112 degrees 51 minutes west longitude). Winter was approaching, though, so the ships turned around and headed back east until they found a harbor where they could safely overwinter. Soon the Arctic temperatures turned the harbor's water to ice, and Parry's ships were frozen into place there. Parry described the sounds the ships made as they became trapped in ice:

A great squeezing of the young floes took place.... The noise it makes when heard at a distance very much resembles that of a heavy waggon labouring over a deep gravelly road; but when a nearer approach is made, it is more like the growling of wild animals, for which it was in one or two instances mistaken. It was however rather useful than otherwise to encourage the belief that bears were abroad, as, without some such idea, people are apt to become careless about going armed.

Parry and his crew built a hut on shore, and lived there as well as on the ships during the winter months. It was a very difficult winter for Parry and his men. Just as the sun never sets during the Arctic summer season, it never rises during the Arctic winter, and the party lived in constant nighttime, never seeing the sun for

Arctic Hibernation

Some animals, such as raccoons, skunks, and groundhogs, spend the winter in a very deep sleep called *hibernation*. During this time their body temperatures drop, they breathe very slowly, and they don't wake up until spring comes. Hibernating animals can easily die if they become too cold. That's why you won't find very many animals in the Arctic that hibernate. One creature that does is the carabid beetle. While most Arctic insects die during the winter, this beetle can survive temperatures as low as −40° F (−40° C).

Polar bears don't really hibernate, but they do spend the winter months inside dens, where they spend most of the time sleeping. During these months the females deliver their cubs, who then snooze along with them as they nurse.

Whales, seals, and fish don't hibernate, either. In fact, they just continue with their lives. The whales congregate in open areas of water, which are kept from freezing by strong ocean currents. Seals live under the ice, coming up to breathe through small holes they keep open by shoving away ice as it forms.

Publish Your Own Newspaper

Parry and his crew created their own newspaper during their first winter in the Arctic. Written and read by the men onboard the ship, it was published every Monday for 22 months, beginning on November 1, 1819. The *North Georgia Gazette and Winter Chronicle* featured poems, essays, articles, and jokes. You can publish your own newspaper, just as Parry did. Do it all by yourself, or get your friends and family involved, too— it's up to you.

Materials

Adult supervision required

Several sheets of 11 × 17-inch paper

Ruler

Pencil

Black marker

Glue stick

Photos or pictures cut out from magazines

1. Come up with a name for your newspaper. You might want to name it after yourself, your family, your town—maybe even your dog!
2. What do you want to include in your newspaper? You could write a story or a poem. You could put in some jokes, or a weather report. You might want to include an interview with somebody— maybe your mom, dad, or best friend. How about a review of your favorite movie or book? The more pages your newspaper has, the more you can include in it. Try to have at least 8 or 10 articles for your newspaper—you can write them all, or you can ask your friends or family to contribute some. Come up with short headlines, or titles, for each article.
3. Fold one or more (depending on how many newspaper pages you want) sheets of 11 × 17-inch paper in half, so that your newspaper pages will be 8½ × 11 inches. Each 11 × 17-inch sheet of paper makes 4 newspaper pages, because both the front and the back of the paper will be used. Next, design your newspaper's layout. Use the ruler and the pencil to measure out and draw sections on each page, in which you will write your articles and paste your pictures. You can make all of the sections the same size, or you can play around with different sizes. Think about how much space each article or picture is going to need. Don't forget to leave a space at the top of the first page for your newspaper's title!
4. When you are happy with your layout, use the marker to print your newspaper's title at the top of the first page. Use the pencil to neatly print each article in a separate section. The headline of each article should be slightly larger and darker than the article itself, to help it stand out. Next, glue your pictures into their sections. You can then go back and erase the lines that you drew to make the sections if you want to.
5. Ask an adult to make photocopies of your newspaper. Give copies to your family and friends—even your teacher.

months. It was bitterly cold, too: temperatures reached as low as –55° F (– 48° C). The sun finally reappeared in February, but it would still be months before the ice melted and they could travel again. Normally this happens around June, but this particular winter was longer than normal, and the ships remained frozen in the harbor until August 1. That year (1820), the Arctic had its spring and summer all in one month— August—and then fall began! There wasn't time to explore more new territory before winter set in again. Although Parry was unhappy about that, he had already accomplished a great deal. No one had ever mapped as much new land as Parry did during this voyage.

After returning to England in 1820, Parry launched a second expedition in the spring of 1821. Again he went in search of the Northwest Passage, this time taking a more southerly route. On this voyage Parry and his men explored the Melville Peninsula, and they spent two winters in the Arctic. As they had on their previous journey, they traded food and supplies with native people, whom Parry called the Esquimaux, that they encountered on their journey. He wrote about these encounters in his ship's log:

> While thus employed we heard voices inshore, which we soon knew to be those of some Esquimaux coming off to us. Shortly after, several canoes made their appearance; and seventeen of these people came alongside the *Fury*. Having hauled their kayaks (canoes) upon the floe, they began to barter their commodities, consisting of seal and whale blubber, whale-bone, spears, lines, and the skins of the seal, bear, fox, deer, and dog. Our first endeavour was to procure as much oil as possible, of which, as we had been informed by the Hudson's Bay ships, several tons are thus almost annually obtained from these people. We soon found that they had been well accustomed to bargain-making, for it was with some difficulty that we could prevail upon them to sell the oil for any thing of reasonable value. They frequently gave us to understand that they wanted saws and harpoons in exchange for it, and as these were articles which we could not spare, it was not without trouble that we obtained, in the course of the evening, two barrels of blubber in exchange for several knives, large nails, and pieces of iron hoop, which was certainly a dear bargain on our side. If they saw more than one of these at a time, they would try hard to get the whole for the commodity they were offering, though, when we had for some time persisted in refusing, they would not only accept what was offered, but jump for joy at having obtained it.

Parry did not find the passage he sought, and he returned to England in 1823. He persisted in his exploration efforts, seeking the Northwest Passage again on a 1824–1825 voyage, where he explored Prince Regent Inlet as well as other areas.

On his fourth and last Arctic expedition, Parry's goal was not to find the Northwest Passage, but to reach the North Pole. Departing in 1827, he proceeded northeast along Spitsbergen. On this journey he brought along *sledges*, 20-foot-long boats that had attachable wheels as well as sails. These boats were heavy and slow, but their design enabled Parry and his men to travel over whatever combination of land and open water the Arctic offered. As Parry had discovered during earlier expeditions, the Arctic terrain is very unpredictable. Temperatures, storms, and other factors can result in a lot of ice, but they can just as easily result in a lot of

Northern Names

While some places in the Arctic were named after the Europeans who discovered them, others were named after some feature of the land or its inhabitants. Some names are just plain odd! Here are a few examples of the colorful names of places in the Arctic and subarctic.

Drowning, Ontario, Canada

Bear Island, Russia

Forget, Quebec, Canada

Moose Factory, Ontario, Canada

Snare River, Northwest Territories

Killala Lake, Ontario, Canada

Umbozero, Russia

Lovozero, Russia

Igloolik, Northwest Territories

open water. It was certainly to Parry's advantage that he could now cover both with relative ease. Using the sledges, he and his crew traveled farther north than anyone ever had before—82 degrees 45 minutes north latitude, or within 500 miles of the Geographic North Pole. His record held for nearly 50 years.

Parry's Arctic career was considered a tremendous success, and the books he wrote about his voyages were well received.

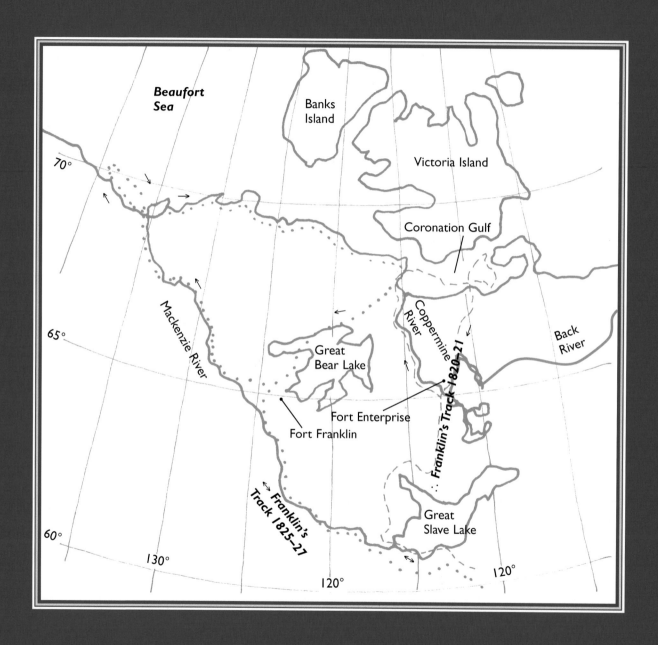

5

John Franklin Leads Arctic Exploration's Biggest Disaster, 1845–1847

Between Sir William Parry's last voyage of 1827 and John Franklin's most famous one from 1845 to 1847, the British government mounted just two major expeditions. Neither captured the enthusiasm of the British public, and both bordered on disaster.

The Long Journey of Sir John Ross

The first of those two voyages was made in 1829 and led by Sir John Ross, a well-known Scottish explorer whose first expedition in search of the Northwest Passage had proved unsuccessful—and embarrassing. As he entered Lancaster Sound in 1818, Ross saw a range of

This map shows the routes of two early Franklin expeditions.

Ice Mirages

Ice mirages have been seen by explorers in both the Arctic and Antarctic. Voyagers have reported spotting what look like castles or whole islands that, when approached, turned out not to be there at all. The illusions often resemble giant icebergs sailing slowly across the sky, or icy mountains hanging upside down.

Their cause is temperature differences, which distort light rays. When the air just above the ground is either very much colder or very much hotter than the air higher up, light is bent and a mirage is created. What's seen is a distorted reflection of what really is usually the sky, clouds, or an iceberg.

mountains blocking the passageway. His crewmen argued that they did not see the mountains and urged him to continue, but Ross insisted that the ship travel no farther into the sound. The next year, William Parry sailed through Lancaster Sound, proving that John Ross had been mistaken. The mountains that had led him to end his exploration of Lancaster Sound did not really exist at all: John Ross had been fooled by a *mirage*

This map shows the route of Franklin's last expedition.

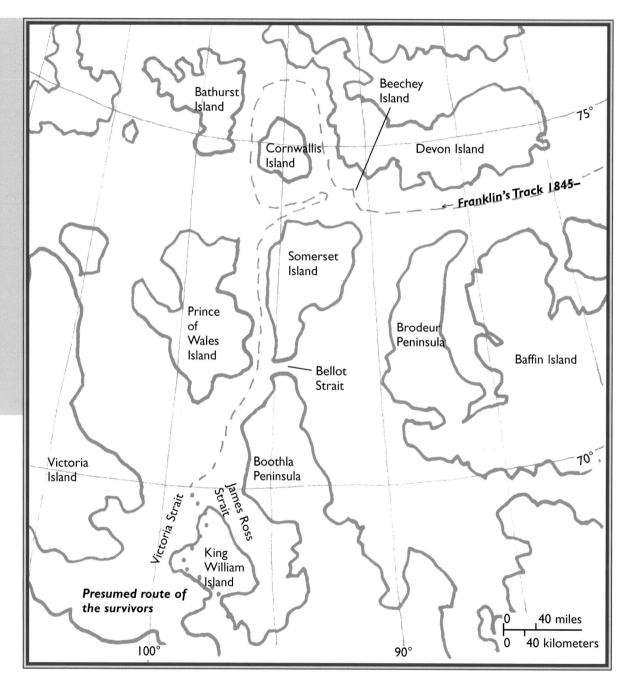

A Field Guide to Ice

People who visit the Arctic are often amazed at the many types of ice it has to offer. Here are some of the most often seen ice types.

Coast ice: This ice can be very thick and is attached to and near the shoreline.

Pancake ice: Pancake ice is thin and very flat and is the first layer of ice that freezes. It lies in pieces like separate pancakes, which can be up to 15 inches across.

Sludge ice: This is slushy ice that ships can pass right through.

Young ice: Ice that has recently formed at the shore. As it thickens it becomes pancake ice.

Drift ice: Large flat pieces of ice that are up to two feet thick. Drift ice floats throughout Arctic waters.

Bergy bits: Pieces of ice that range from the size of a boulder up to that of a house, these are moved through the ocean by water currents. They are called "bits" only because they are small compared to full-sized icebergs.

Growlers: Larger than bergy bits, these icebergs grind against a ship's hull, causing a sound that resembles a growl. This kind of ice tends to move with water currents as well.

Pack ice: Sea ice that has formed into a mass and that is not attached to land. Pack ice is moved by wind currents.

Hummocky floes: These are ice chunks with a thick layer of snow on top.

Pressure ridges: These are the "car wrecks" of the ice world. One large slab of ice is forced up over another, or two slabs have been forced together, creating ridges. These ridges can be up to 40 feet high and extend in a line for many miles, making it extremely difficult to drag sleds and supplies up and over them.

John Franklin in a *daguerreotype*, an early form of photograph.

Inlet, where disaster struck. The *Victory* became trapped in the ice, forcing Ross and his crew to spend four years in the Arctic. They lived both on the ship and in a hut on land over the winters. By July 1832, Ross and some of the crew decided to launch the small boats they'd brought along onto the shallow water that was pooled over the steadfast ice. The men were facing starvation, and they hoped that a passing ship might spot them. It was their only hope of surviving.

(an optical illusion). This was very unfortunate for Ross. For one thing, it was very embarrassing. Even worse, had he only continued traveling through Lancaster Sound, he might have realized that it is indeed a route to the Northwest Passage!

In 1829 Ross convinced one of his friends to finance another expedition to the Arctic. Traveling on a steamship called the *Victory*, he and his crew sailed deep into Canada's Northwest Territories. They sailed into Prince Regent

The last message found from the Franklin Expedition.

For months, Ross and the men who had joined him barely survived in their tiny boats. Finally, they spotted a ship in the distance. Rescue! The ship almost passed them by (small boats are easy to miss in the vast Arctic ice and sea), but Ross and his men were found and taken aboard the vessel. Ross and his men were so close to death from starvation that they were unrecognizable. It was 1833, and they had been in the Arctic for four years. Who were their amazed rescuers? The rest of Ross's crew on his own ship, which had eventually managed to make it home—and were back in the Arctic on another voyage!

The Expedition of George Back

The next expedition was launched in 1837 under George Back, who also sought the Northwest Passage. On Back's expedition toward the Kent Peninsula, in the west Arctic, his ship was so squeezed by the ice that the bolts popped out of the wood, the deck heaved, and the turpentine used as caulking between the timbers was forced out and dripped down the sides of the ship. Back and his men raced for home. They made it to safety, and the ship was repaired when the ice eased.

Although the British Admiralty was losing enthusiasm for Arctic exploration, whaling, fur trading, and other industries continued to thrive there; the Arctic was hardly an abandoned area. There were regular contacts with the native peoples, too. But only a few hundred miles of the Arctic Ocean and its lands remained unmapped. It seemed less and less likely that a Northwest Passage existed at all.

The Franklin Expedition

By the 1840s, however, the British decided to try again. John Franklin (1786–1847) was an experienced Arctic explorer who had served on and commanded polar voyages in 1818, 1819–1822, and 1825–1827. During these voyages he gained a reputation for his mapping skills, as well as for his analyses of water depths, speeds, currents, and tides in the Arctic. He was accordingly given a new mission by the British Admiralty: find the Northwest Passage.

Franklin's trip began in 1845. His orders were very specific: reach Greenland, cross Baffin Bay, go through Lancaster Sound to Barrow Strait's western end, proceed south for what was thought to be the final 500 unmapped miles to the mainland of North America, steer west along its northern coast to the Bering Strait and the Pacific Ocean—and thus prove the existence of a Northwest Passage between the Atlantic and Pacific Oceans.

His ships, the *Erebus* and the *Terror*, were state-of-the-art vessels designed for polar voyages. Each weighed more than 300 tons and stretched more than 100 feet long, and their timbers were reinforced from 10 inches up to eight feet thick in various areas to guard against the ice. They even had, in places, cast iron for extra strength and cork for insulation. The ships also contained steam boilers, coal bunkers, and extra steam engines as well as retractable

A painting of Franklin's ships, the *Erebus* and the *Terror*, in an Antarctic storm (note the penguins that indicate this).

Finding the Direction to the North Pole

Direction-finding devices can break, fall into glacier crevasses, or splash into the Arctic waters, and compasses do not work if they are near the Magnetic North Pole. If the Franklin expedition had just four sticks among their supplies, they would have fared better than they did. Do this activity on a sunny day, any time except noon (when it is difficult to see shadows).

1. Measure and cut or saw the sticks to make them of equal length (at least 2 feet). Cut the sticks so that they have reasonably flat tops.
2. Push the first stick into the ground at an angle, tilting it slightly until you can see a long shadow. Leave it there, securely poked into the ground.
3. Write the letter W on a small piece of masking tape. Put this label on the second stick. Place the second stick in the ground exactly where the first stick's shadow ends.
4. Wait one to two hours.
5. Write the letter E on another small piece of masking tape and attach it to the third stick. Push this stick into the ground at the end of where the shadow is now. (As the sun moves across the sky, the shadow will move, too.) Leave the other sticks where they are. The line that runs from the E (or east) stick to the W (or west) stick is a line that runs east–west.

Materials

Adult supervision required
Tape measure or yardstick
Knife or saw
4 sturdy sticks (such as dowels, croquet sticks, or yardsticks) that are each at least 2 feet long
Pen, pencil, or marker

Masking tape
3-inch-long piece of string
Patch of dirt or sand where sticks can be stuck into the ground without shadows from other objects interfering

6. To find the line that runs north–south, make a loop in one end of the string and tie it to the top of the fourth stick. Trim the other end of the string so that the length is a little shorter than the distance between the W and the E sticks. Then tie the end to the top of the E stick.
7. Hold the fourth stick securely and with the string kept taut. Walk in a circle around the E stick, using the fourth stick to scratch the circle on the ground. Using the same length of string (be sure to keep it taut), do the same around the W stick.
8. Using the fourth stick as a tool, poke two holes in the ground, one at each end of the two points where the two circles intersect.
9. Stand in front of all three sticks so that the W stick is to your left and the E stick is to your right. Put the fourth stick in the ground in the new hole closest to you. Mark this stick S.
10. Pull up your first stick (the only one that doesn't have masking tape on it) and put it into the other hole at the other intersecting point. Label it N. Tie the string to the S and N sticks, making sure it's taut. This is the north–south line. Now you know which way is North—all thanks to the sun!

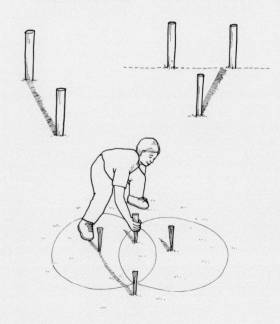

Finding the direction to the North Pole.

£20,000 Sterling (100,000 DOLLARS,) REWARD.

TO BE GIVEN by her Britannic Majesty's Government to such a private Ship, or distributed among such private Ships, of any Country, as may, in the judgment of the Board of Admiralty, have rendered efficient assistance to

SIR JOHN FRANKLIN, HIS SHIPS, or their Crews,

and may have contributed directly to extricate them from the Ice.

H. G. WARD,
SECRETARY TO THE ADMIRALTY.
LONDON, 23rd MARCH, 1849.

The attention of WHALERS, or any other Ships disposed to aid in this service, is particularly directed to SMITH'S SOUND and JONES'S SOUND, in BAFFIN'S BAY, to REGENT's INLET and the GULF of BOOTHIA, as well as to any of the Inlets or Channels leading out of BARROW'S STRAIT, or the Sea beyond, either Northward or Southward.

VESSELS Entering through BEHRING'S STRAITS would necessarily direct their search North and South of MELVILLE ISLAND.

NOTE.—Persons desirous of obtaining Information relative to the Missing Expedition, which has not been heard of since JULY, 1845, are referred to EDMUND A. GRATTAN, Esq., Her Britannic Majesty's Consul, BOSTON, MASSACHUSETTS : or, ANTHONY BARCLAY, Esq., Her Majesty's Consul, NEW YORK.

Reward poster seeking help for Franklin and his men.

propellers and detachable rudders, which could come in handy if a ship encountered ice.

The officers and crew were to receive very high pay because of the dangers of Arctic travel—more than three times what crewmen earned at home—and they all became quite famous even before they left. People were excited about this expedition. Strangers bought the sailors drinks at pubs, and huge parties were held for the officers.

Although space was always tight on a ship, the comfort of the crew and officers was a priority. They had a stove near their bunks, board games, one of the new daguerreotype cameras (*daguerreotype* is an early form of photography that produced photographs on a silver or silver-covered copper plate), and a desalinator (which makes sea water drinkable by removing the salt). They even had a dog named Neptune and a pet monkey named Jacko on the ship for entertainment. And there was plenty of food—enough to last for three years. Ten thousand people waved and cheered to the men as the ships sailed out of the harbor on May 19, 1845. Never had an expedition party been so well equipped or well prepared. Surely success lay ahead!

By winter, however, five men had changed their minds about the voyage and found another ship to take them home. Three crewmen had died of unknown causes, and Franklin had made one navigational error based on a mistake in the maps.

The ships forged ahead. During the second winter, however, 21 more men died. Franklin was among them. The cause of his death was mysterious—although he was 61 years old, he had never been in poor health. What had killed him? And what had killed the other men whose deaths could not be explained?

Worse was yet to come for the remaining men in John Franklin's expedition. Sailing between Victoria and King William Islands, both ships became trapped in crushing sea ice. By the spring of 1847, the trapped crew was getting low on food, and the ice showed no signs of melting. They decided to leave the ship (for it was lost to the ice) and set out on foot in search of rescue. The men had only the food they could carry, and they had no sleds, tents, or adequately warm clothing. Starving and ill-protected from the bitter cold, all members of the party died.

Britain, under much pressure from Lady Franklin, John Franklin's wife, sent dozens of ships in 32 separate expeditions to find Franklin and his crew. Although much of the Arctic was mapped during these searches, many men died during these voyages—and no one found Franklin or his party alive.

The British government must not have been very optimistic about rescuing Franklin or his crew: in 1854 the following announcement was made:

By Admiralty Order, 18 January 1854: It is directed that if they are not heard of previous to 31 March 1854, the Officers & Ships companies are to be removed from the Navy List & are to be considered as having died in the service. Wages are to be paid to their Relatives to that date; as of 1 April 1854, all books and papers are to be dispensed with.

—Admiralty Order No. 263.

Tookoolito and the *Polaris* Expedition

The American *Polaris* expedition, led by Charles Francis Hall, was one of many mounted to search for John Franklin and his men. It would prove to be one of the strangest journeys in history.

Hall and his crew sailed out of Manhattan in August 1871. They were accompanied by Tookoolito (1838–1876), an Inuit native of Baffin Island, and her husband, Ebierbing, both of whom had previously traveled with Hall as guides and interpreters. Within five months of setting sail, however, Hall was dead. People suspected that a member of his own crew had poisoned him. Then the ship became stuck in deadly ice. For two years, the crew lived onboard the ship, waiting for the ice to thaw. Finally, the *Polaris* began to break under the stress of the ice. The crew headed for land. As they were moving supplies onto the land, they noticed something very odd. They were drifting away from the ship! The "land" they had escaped to was actually a large, floating piece of ice (an *ice floe*) about four miles in circumference. Eighteen people—nine American crewmen, two Inuit couples (including Tookoolito and her husband), and five Inuit children—found themselves stranded on the floe. Some of them weren't even wearing coats. All they had were the small boats and the little bit of food they'd unloaded from the *Polaris*. Stunned, they watched as the ship slowly disappeared from view.

The Inuit quickly built an igloo village for everyone. Tookoolito's husband managed to kill a few seals for food, but winter had arrived and the group could not find enough to eat. They were slowly starving to death, and they weren't even sure where they were.

For months they drifted on the ice floe. Circumstances were desperate, but Tookoolito's skills and dedication kept the group alive in the face of starvation, disease, storms, freezing cold, and the constant danger of being crushed by drifting ice. Although she could have abandoned the others on several occasions, Tookoolito stayed with them, and it was through her efforts that everyone stayed alive.

Finally, on April 30, 1873, all 18 people were rescued by a passing steamboat. They had spent six and a half months drifting on that piece of ice and had traveled more than 1,500 miles!

The story of Tookoolito and the *Polaris* adventure is an amazing account of danger, courage, and loyalty. You can read more about it in a book for adults titled *Midnight to the North: The Untold Story of the Inuit Woman Who Saved the* Polaris *Expedition*, by Sheila Nickerson (Penguin Putnam Inc., 2002).

In 1859, 14 years after Franklin and his men had set sail for the Arctic, an expedition led by Francis Leopold McClintock discovered human remains on King William Island, as well as a message that had been written by the doomed men.

April 25, 1848. H.M. Ships 'Terror' and 'Erebus' were deserted on the 22nd. April, 5 leagues NNW of this, having been beset since 12 Sept. 1846. The officers and crews consisting of 105 souls under the command of Captain F.R.M. Crozier, landed here in Lat. 69 degrees 37 minutes 42 seconds N. and Long. 98 degrees 41 minutes W. This paper was found by Lt. Irving under the cairn supposed to have been built by Sir James Ross in 1831, 4 miles to the northward, where it had been deposited by the late Commander Gore in June 1847. Sir James Ross' pillar has not however been found, and the paper has been transferred to this position which is that in which Sir J. Ross' pillar was erected. . . . Sir John Franklin died on the 11th June 1847, and the total loss by deaths in the Expedition has been to this date 9 officers and 15 men.

James Fitzjames, Captain, *HMS Erebus*.
FRM Crozier, Captain and Senior Officer and start on tomorrow 26th for Back's Fish River.

Most people agree that this message doesn't make much sense. The writing is confusing, and the men's plan to head for Back's Fish River seems very odd. They were probably near death and not thinking clearly when it was written. And they were never heard from again.

One hundred and forty years later, scientists determined that although they were weakened by starvation, scurvy, and other things, the men had probably been killed either by botulism, a disease that is often caused by eating food that has not been properly canned, or by lead poisoning (at the time, lead cans were used to store food). Trapped in a land of huge icebergs and immense danger, Franklin and his men were killed by one of the smallest organisms in the world.

After the tragedy of the Franklin Expedition, efforts to find the Northwest Passage ceased for a very long time.

From Feast to Famine

Here is a typical week of dinners that Franklin's crew enjoyed before disaster struck their expedition:

Monday: potatoes and salted beef

Tuesday: canned meats and vegetables (there were six to choose from)

Wednesday: salt pork with split peas

Thursday: canned meat with canned vegetables in soups and stews; pudding with dried fruit

Friday: salted beef with cabbage, pickles, or onions

Saturday: salt pork with split peas

Sunday: baked goods with canned meat and vegetables in gravy

In addition, bread, rum, and fresh lemon juice were served every day. The ship's officers ate even better: they had cheese, pasta and rice, fancier canned foods, salted and smoked fish, and, while it lasted, fresh meat and fruit. They also had fancier breads and liquor.

Now take a look at what the men had to eat toward the end of their expedition: deerskin, *lichen* (a not very tasty type of wild plant), animal intestines, and boiled shoe leather.

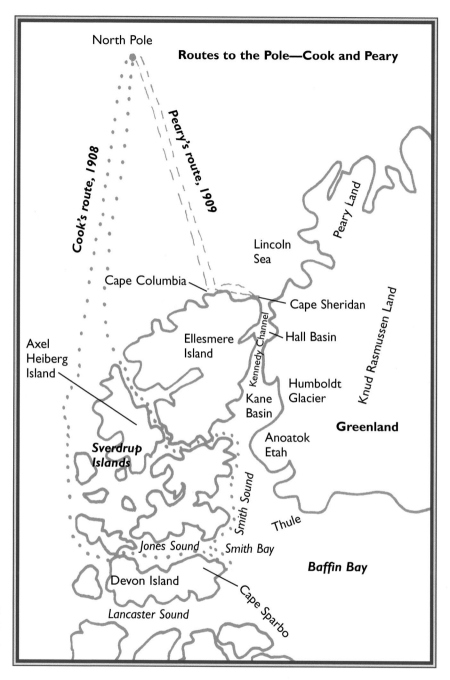

North Pole

Routes to the Pole—Cook and Peary

Cook's route, 1908

Peary's route, 1909

Lincoln Sea

Peary Land

Cape Columbia

Cape Sheridan

Hall Basin

Ellesmere Island

Kennedy Channel

Knud Rasmussen Land

Axel Heiberg Island

Humboldt Glacier

Kane Basin

Greenland

Sverdrup Islands

Anoatok Etah

Smith Sound

Thule

Jones Sound

Smith Bay

Baffin Bay

Devon Island

Cape Sparbo

Lancaster Sound

These are the routes Cook and Peary took toward the North Pole.

pigeons. He died in his attempt. Between 1907 and 1909, an American journalist named Walter Wellman made three attempts to reach the North Pole by motorized blimp. He also failed.

Newspapers began to pay a lot of attention to explorers. In addition to making them famous, this publicity also allowed explorers to raise large amounts of money to finance expeditions. Peary and Cook both received a lot of attention from the press, as well as a lot of money from their supporters. They were famous before their journeys had even begun.

Robert Peary's Expedition to the North Pole

Robert Edwin Peary (1856–1920), a United States Navy engineer, focused his entire life on reaching the North Pole. (Like others, he had what has been called "North Pole mania.") He wanted to conquer the Arctic in order to be well known. Peary wanted to be a big shot all his life. Even when he was just a boy, he told his mother, "Remember, Mother, I *must* have fame!"

Peary's career as an explorer began in 1886, when he traveled to northern Greenland. He returned there in 1893. This time he brought along his wife, Josephine, who was pregnant. Josephine would give birth to their daughter, Marie, in Greenland. The expedition also included a small American crew as well as several Canadian Inuit. Peary knew he needed the skills of these native people to successfully complete his journey, but he treated them very badly. He thought that, being European, he was just naturally "better" than they were, and he looked down on them and called their igloos "smelly." Although his trip was successful, he sure didn't make very many friends along the way.

Between 1898 and 1906 Peary made several unsuccessful attempts to reach the North Pole. He raised the money for these trips by giving speeches about his travels. Peary was a popular speaker—he once gave 165 speeches in just four months—and he even appeared in Buffalo Bill's Wild West Show. The Arctic voyages took their toll on Peary—he lost most of his toes to frostbite, and he sometimes had to wrap himself in the American flag he had with him to help protect him from the cold. But Peary was always looking for ways to gain money and fame. He took chunks of a huge meteorite that had landed in the Arctic and sold them to the American Museum of Natural History in New York. (The Inuit put the meteorite to more practical use: they chipped off pieces of the iron-rich rock to use as spearheads for their harpoons.) Peary even brought back both dead and living Inuit and put them on display in New York. All of the living Inuit soon died.

On July 6, 1908, Peary embarked on his eighth and most famous expedition. He named one of his ships the *Roosevelt* in honor of Theodore Roosevelt, who was president of the United States at the time. President Roosevelt came to see him off, as did thousands of other well-wishers. His crew of six Americans included the African American Matthew Henson, whom he called "my body servant." Later, during the journey, he would add to his group several native people.

Peary and his group stayed in Greenland over the winter. While he was there, some Inuit people told him that another explorer, Frederick Cook, had come through seven months earlier, headed for the North Pole. Peary was shocked. If that was true, there was no way that Peary would beat Cook to the North Pole unless something very bad happened to him. But he decided to continue his journey. Who knew if Cook would make it?

Peary seemed to remain in very good spirits despite the news about Cook. He even put on a Christmas celebration for his group and the local Inuit. They had races, wrestling and boxing matches, and other activities, and Christmas dinner featured musk ox, plum pudding, champagne, and other delicacies. Six Inuit women put on a dance show as well.

Spring came, and Peary continued to travel to the North Pole. He decided to take only five people with him—four Inuit men (their names were Ootah, Egingwah, Seegloos, and Ooqueach) and Matthew Henson. The rest of his group

Commander Robert E. Peary, 1909, in the garments he wore to the North Pole.

stayed behind in Greenland. Why did he specifically choose these people? He wanted to be the only white man to reach the North Pole! During this leg of the trip, Peary was very lax about taking measurements to determine their location, although he boasted that they averaged 26 miles per day of progress north. Years later he admitted—after Matthew Henson had already revealed

Measuring Longitude

Longitude, one's position from east to west, was just as important for polar explorers as latitude, the position from south to north. Look at any globe to see the precise march of the imaginary lines that hug the planet vertically. Those are the longitude lines.

It even sounds somewhat easy to determine one's longitude: on the Greenwich, England, line (called the prime meridian), which is arbitrarily designated as zero longitude, the sun reaches its highest place in the sky at noon. (This is true on any day, whether it is summer when the noon sun is high or winter when the noon sun is low—every day the sun reaches its highest point at noon.) Before leaving, explorers set a clock to Greenwich Mean Time, or the time in Greenwich. Then they just keep that clock handy, to check it at the Sun's highest peak wherever they are. If the Greenwich clock said 11:20 A.M., the difference between that time and noon where they are is 40 minutes. The explorer then divided 40 minutes by 4 (4 is always the number to use), and got the result, 10. Presto: the ship was at 10 degrees longitude (*west* longitude, of course, when the ship was going west across the Atlantic Ocean).

There is, however, one problem. Clocks never used to be that accurate! A couple of minutes fast or slow, maybe even slower on foggy days when the dampness got into the gears, maybe faster when a huge storm tossed the ship around a bit—all this could add up and change the clock's time. It could force a navigator into making a mistake—which could easily mean being a thousand miles off from the longitude where he thought he was. The navigator, looking at all the maps available, and having the longitude wrong, could think the ship was approaching the Marquesas Islands but in fact, it could be a completely new land elsewhere.

For example, in the 1600s a Spanish expedition discovered the Solomon Islands—which no European power had claimed to date—but thought they were the same old Marquesas Islands, so they didn't claim them. Instead, France claimed them later. King Philip II of Spain was furious!

Soon Spain, France, and Britain were all offering big cash prizes for the invention of an accurate clock. That would make longitude measurements accurate, too. They set the rule that on the long trip from Europe to the West Indies, the clock was allowed to be only two minutes off, *total*. That way, the longitude would be very, very accurate.

Years later, in 1775, after several tries, an English carpenter named John Harrison finally collected the prize for an accurate clock. Ships could accurately keep track of their longitude from that point on.

it in his own memoirs—that from 87 degrees 47 minutes north latitude on (about 133 miles from the pole), Peary made no measurements at all.

On April 6, 1909, Peary announced his expedition's arrival at the North Pole. Ootah, one of the four Inuit who had accompanied him, commented, "There is nothing here . . . just ice." This was true.

But when Peary returned to Greenland the next year, he was informed that he had not been the first man to reach the North Pole. Frederick Cook claimed to have reached it the year before Peary did, in 1908. Although Cook had left notes about the measurements he had taken with a hunter on his way back (as "proof" that he had made it to the North Pole), Peary believed that Cook was lying, and he sent telegrams around the world claiming that he was the first man to set foot at the North Pole.

Frederick Cook Heads North

Frederick Albert Cook (1865–1940), an American doctor, loved the beauty of the Arctic as much as he loved the thrill of conquering it. Like Peary, Cook gave speeches to raise money for his expeditions. He even brought along some Inuit from Greenland on his speaking tour. Cook also launched the first-ever Arctic tour cruises for the paying public in 1893 and 1894.

The Furriest Animal Alive

Musk oxen, big and shaggy as buffaloes, are the furriest animals alive. An adult musk ox's fur can be six inches deep, or even more. This protects them from the Arctic cold. For winter their brown overcoats (the fur that you see) grow thick and hang straight to the ground. The animals also grow thick, silky-soft undercoats (the fur next to their skin) that are eight times warmer than a sheep's wool.

These creatures are Ice Age mammals. They are relatives of wild cattle and of goats, although their curved horns and beards make them look more like water buffaloes. Native people call them *oomingmak* ("bearded one"). They travel in herds, moving in groups of 8 to 15 along the Arctic and subarctic's low-lying plains and river valleys, and they eat plants. Although food is difficult for them to find in the winter, they eat so much during the summer and fall that they survive until the next spring.

Adults weigh 600 to 700 pounds. They are very strong—an adult musk ox can break a sheet of ice by dropping its heavy head onto it. They have very good eyesight, even at night.

Frederick Cook en route.

These cruises were for tourists, not explorers, and the people who went on them were allowed to shoot the wild animals they saw on the journey. They did this for fun, not for food—they wanted to say they had been brave enough to kill a polar bear all by themselves. (Of course, the polar bear didn't have a gun, so it wasn't a very fair fight!)

By the summer of 1907, Cook set out to reach the North Pole. He kept very quiet about it, unlike Peary, who worked hard to get as much publicity as possible before he set out for the North Pole. Cook began his journey with nine Inuit men. While Peary looked down on the Inuit, Cook treated these men with great respect. Also in Cook's party were one white American man and 105 dogs. The group brought along 11 dogsleds.

When they reached 81 degrees 38 minutes north latitude, Cook selected two of the Inuit—Ahwelah and Etukishook—to come with him on the final leg of the trip. Along the way he took a lot of latitude and longitude measurements. They made good progress, and by the spring of 1908 they were close to the North Pole. Starting at noon on April 21, 1908, he took measurements every six hours, using his watch and his compass, as well as a *sextant* (a tool used to navigate by the stars) and a *chronometer*, a special kind of clock that keeps very accurate time. These were the most accurate tools to measure latitude and longitude at the time. At midnight on April 22, he believed he was just one-half mile from the North Pole. The next day, he noted that his tent pole's shadow was the same length all day long—another indication that he was very close to "true north." On April 23, 1908, Cook claimed he'd reached the top of the world—the North Pole. He then headed back south. Along the

way he named two islands after his two Inuit companions.

During the long trip back, Cook was told that Peary was close to reaching the North Pole. He left his own measurements with a local polar bear hunter as proof that he had been the first to make it there, then caught a ship back to the Shetland Islands. From there he sent a telegram to the International Polar Commission saying that he'd reached the North Pole. He also wrote a 2,000-word story and sent it to the *New York Herald*, another big newspaper in New York. He told the people at the newspaper that they could buy his story for $3,000. They did.

In his story Cook said that the land he saw on his journey had all been flat areas of snow and ice. Some people wondered about this: if he had really been where he said he was, he should have also seen several huge, hilly islands. Peary jumped at the chance to publicly accuse Cook of lying about having reached the North Pole. Cook was angry about this, and the battle over who was lying and who was telling the truth began. Newspapers ran big stories about the controversy, and both Peary and Cook went on tour to give speeches. Each said that he was the first to reach the North Pole. Both said that the other man was a liar. In the end, more people believed Peary than Cook, but many others believed that *both* of them were lying.

The Legacy of Peary and Cook

Many people had very strong opinions about Peary and Cook themselves, as well as about their claims to have been the first to reach the North Pole. A popular expression at the time was "Cook is a liar and a gentleman and Peary is neither." The mystery of who had reached the North Pole first was never answered, but several things are certain: Peary did not take enough measurements during his journey, and Cook's measurements were not always accurate. Neither of them had brought along a witness who was trained to know if they were really at the North Pole. Were Peary and Cook just careless, or were they trying to pull the wool over people's eyes? It's difficult to say, but by the 1930s most geographers agreed that both of them had been at least 100 miles away from the North Pole. Still, that didn't stop both men from becoming famous. But Matthew Henson, Peary's African American assistant, did not become famous at all, even though he had come just as close to the North Pole as Peary had. Just as the white Europeans paid no attention to the accomplishments of the native Inuit, they paid no attention to the accomplishments of an African American. Henson ended up working as a parking lot attendant and messenger in New York City. He died in 1955 at the age of 88, having outlived both Peary and Cook by many years.

Make a Chart of the Explorers' Top Latitudes

Many explorers tried to be the first to reach the farthest north—the highest latitude. You can see how far the explorers came by making a chart to show their top latitudes.

1. Make a rough draft of your chart. Using a pencil and a ruler, draw a straight line all the way up the width of the paper, on the far left side. At the bottom of the line, write "40° N." This indicates 40 degrees north latitude, which is a bit farther south than any European city from which the explorers in this book began their voyages.

2. Move up the line about an inch, and write "50° N" there. Move up an inch and write "60° N." Continue doing this until you have written a line for 90 degrees north latitude (the North Pole).

3. Now draw a straight line across the length of your paper, at the top. Starting at the left side of this line, write the year 980. Move just a little bit to the right (less than a quarter-inch) and write the year 1000. Move about an inch to the right and write the year 1100. Continue writing down centuries—1200, 1300, and so on—all the way up to the year 2000. Space each year that you write about an inch from the one before it.

4. In the spaces between centuries, mark little lines to represent periods of 10 years.

5. Go through the chapters that you've read so far. On a separate piece of paper, write down each explorer's name, the year of his voyage to the North Pole, and the highest latitude he reached.

6. Once you have all of this information, you can add it to your chart. Find the explorer's highest latitude reached on the vertical line, then look at the horizontal line to find the year of his voyage. Right where the two lines intersect, write the explorer's name vertically.

7. Copy your chart onto large poster board, using a different colored pencil or marker for each explorer's information.

Pituffik (Thule Air Base)

Baffin Bay

Coast of Greenland

Greenland

Illorsuit

Disko Island

Uummannaq

• Ilulissat

• Kangerlussuaq

8

Gretel Ehrlich Explores Greenland's Nature and Its Native Peoples, 1993–2000

Since Peary and Cook's race to the North Pole, Arctic exploration has taken many avenues. Important trends include novel ways of getting there, respectful study of the Inuit and their culture, a focus on the natural history of and science issues related to the Arctic, and the active involvement of women in polar exploration.

Admiral Richard E. Byrd attempted to fly over the North Pole in 1926. He may or may not have succeeded. In 1927 Roald Amundsen probably did fly over it—his vehicle was a blimp. Two American nuclear submarines traveled *under* the ice to reach the North Pole in the late 1950s, and Ralph Plaisted made it there by snowmobile in 1968. In 1969 Wally Herbert used a dogsled to

Some of the places where Ehrlich stayed on the coast of Greenland.

follow Peary's route; he may well have been the first person to reach the North Pole by land. Seeking another first, a man named Naomi Uemura was the first to make it to the North Pole alone, in 1978. By 1991 the *Soyuz*, a Russian submarine, approached the North Pole underwater. This nuclear-powered submarine/icebreaker then forced its way up *through* the ice. Once it was on top of the ice, small boats and a helicopter were used to take the submarine's passengers the rest of the way to the North Pole. One hundred tourists paid about $30,000 each to be part of this three-week trip. There have been many other firsts in Arctic exploration, and Arctic tourism has continued to grow.

Cook's respectful approach toward the Inuit people led others to explore the Arctic's native people and their cultures. From 1910 until the 1920s Knud Rasmussen, a man of both Inuit and Danish ancestry, traveled the Arctic by dogsled for years at a time, stopping in dozens of villages along the way, taking notes on the beliefs, songs, and lifestyles of the different groups of the Inuit people.

The Canadians, most notably Vilhjalmur Stefansson, also studied and recorded the customs of Arctic natives. From 1908 to 1918, he gathered important information and remapped large areas of the Arctic. In the late 1930s a French adventurer, Gontran de Poncins, traveled the Arctic and then wrote a book about his encounters

Nunavut

Canada's newest province, Nunavut, was established on April 1, 1999, for the benefit of native peoples. Nunavut means "our land." Nunavut's territory is a 770,000-square-mile swatch of what was once Arctic Canada.

with the Inuit. His book is called *Kabloona* (the word many Inuit use for "white man"). The 1950s–1970s found French anthropologist Jean Malaurie living with and filming documentaries of the native people, and he wrote a book about them called *The Last Kings of Thule*. The books that explorers wrote during this time are very important, because they preserved the history of the Inuit people for all time. Encounters with white explorers and tourists forever changed the culture of the Inuit. They now hunt by snowmobile, watch television, and live in houses. Many of the old Inuit traditions and ways of living have completely disappeared.

Three of the best writers about the Arctic and its people are Barry Lopez, Hugh Brody, and Gretel Ehrlich. They have each spent years learning about the Arctic and the Inuit, and they write with great sensitivity to, and respect for, the land and its people. Science has always

been part of Arctic exploration, and for the last 100 years or so it has been a major focus of explorers. The polar ocean is probed regularly to monitor its changes in temperature. The aurora borealis (also called the northern lights) are amazing shows of light and color in the Arctic night sky. Scientists study the aurora borealis to see how particles and energy from the sun create these natural electrical extravaganzas. (For more information about the aurora borealis, see the Chapter 13 sidebar titled "The Aurora Australis.") Scientists also study Arctic animals and plants. Even the world's most northerly volcano, on Jan Mayen Island, has been studied. And a group of scientists from many different countries is currently drilling down into the deep ice of central Greenland to look for evidence of climate changes in the Arctic. This is very important information to know if we are ever to understand global warming.

Women in the Arctic

Over the last 50 years or so, women have finally taken their place among Arctic adventurers and experts. In 1955 Louise Arner Boyd, a photographer, reached the North Pole by plane. Beginning in the 1950s, the cultural anthropologist Catherine McClellan gathered a great deal of oral history on the Inuit. By 1988 a 50-year-old New Zealander named Helen Thayer became the first woman to ski alone to the Magnetic

North Pole; she was accompanied only by her dog Charlie, a black husky. She returned to the Magnetic North Pole in 1992 with her husband, Bill, who was 65 years old. They became the oldest explorers (and the first married couple) to reach the North Pole on foot without having extra supplies dropped to them by plane or helicopter. And explorer-writer Ann Bancroft became the first woman to reach the Geographic North Pole in 1986.

Gretel Ehrlich Helps Preserve the Arctic

Gretel Ehrlich is a great example of how some of today's best explorers are actually writers. Her books highlight the nature, scenery, animals, light, and other aspects of the places she visits. Ehrlich also focuses on the people who live in the lands she explores. For her book *This Cold Heaven: Seven Seasons in Greenland*, she lived closely with Inuit, Danish, and other people as she explored Greenland. She carefully researches the people and their cultures that she writes about, from the very first people who reached Greenland about 5,000 years ago, to the Saqqaq Inuit of 2000–1500 B.C., to the Dorset Inuit of about 800 B.C. to A.D. 800, to the Thule Inuit who arrived about A.D. 1050 and who still live there.

For her book *This Cold Heaven*, Ehrlich traveled to several Inuit settlements that had been explored by Knud Rasmussen between 1902 and 1933. Rasmussen wrote about the lives of the native people he encountered while he was there. Ehrlich quotes from his journals, describes his affinity for the Arctic, and tells some of his stories in her own book. During her stays at these settlements, Ehrlich noticed that the Inuit people's lives had changed a great deal since Rasmussen had been there. Her book tells how Inuits today blend the modern world of television, snowmobiles, and grocery stores with their old customs and traditions, such as traveling by dogsled and hunting seal from traditional boats.

Ehrlich writes about places that have been only partly changed by the modern world. She deliberately chooses places where the traditional culture of the people who live there has not entirely disappeared. She has a great deal of respect for the native people who live in the Arctic, but she admits that their ways are sometimes difficult for us in the modern world to agree with. For example, even though she knows that the Inuit depend on the seals and polar bears they kill for food, clothing, and tools, she was very unhappy to see the Inuit kill a mother polar bear who had a small cub with her. But she also had to admit to herself that, as sad as she was about the mother and baby polar bears, she was very happy to be wearing a polar bear parka to keep her warm!

Ehrlich does not just visit Greenland during the summer. She stays there in the endless dark of winter, too. "Up there time comes whole, then is divided into four months of dark, four months of light, and two seasons of twilight when the sun hangs at the horizon as though stuck between two thoughts," she has written.*

While she was visiting Illorsuit, a village on a small island along Baffin Bay, she became very friendly with two Inuit children there—two-year-old Hendrik and six-year-old Maria Louisa. The three of them collected bird eggs to share with the rest of the village and went on many nature hikes. Ehrlich has a special love for all of the villagers she has lived with. But sometimes it's not easy for Ehrlich and the natives to understand each other's language, and Ehrlich uses a dictionary of the local language to help her. Once she looked up the word for "ice." These are all the words that she found: *kaniq, qirihuq, nilak, nilaktaqtuq, hiku, hikuaq, hikuaqtuaq, ilu, hikuiqihuq, hikurhuit, hikuqihuq, hikuliaq, manirak, hikuphinaa, qainnguq, manillat, kassut, iluliaq, ilulissirhuq, auktuq, quihaq, hirmiijaut*. Every one of these words means a different kind of ice: rime frost, freshwater ice, sea ice, thin ice, ice on the inside of the tent, pack ice, new ice, a smooth expanse of ice, the ice edge, solid ice attached to the shore, hummocky ice, pressure ridges, pieces of floating ice, icebergs in the water, melting ice . . .

In *This Cold Heaven*, Ehrlich tells readers about many adventures she had while in Greenland. Once she went with an elder Inuit man on a hunting trip. They were looking for walrus, seal, and narwhal, and they traveled by dogsled. In her book Ehrlich wrote:

When the dogs had rested, we packed up the sleds and headed for home.

It begins with ice and ends with ice. What looks like open water is ice cleared of snow, or else ice blink caused by the shadow of a cloud making frozen water look blue, or sky's reflection of open water turning clouds dark. Sun shone down like a flashlight illuminating a path through pressure ice, a way that had been cleared. Up on the ice cap, the *innerssuit* (beach spirits) and *inorsuit* (glacier spirits) cavorted, coming down to play with our minds. The glacier groaned, its castellated face splintered and calved out thousands of icebergs; the chunk of glacier ice we brought into the tent to melt for tea water exploded.

About another evening, she wrote:

Lying inside my sleeping bag, I listened to the wind. In one day we had prepared a sealskin, eaten polar bear, and hunted Arctic hare. When Jens came back empty-handed, he told stories about the woman who adopted a

Arctic Weather

Which of the following almost never occurs in the Arctic—and why?
    Snowstorms
    High winds
    Lightning
    Rain
    For the answers, see the Selected Answers section in the back of this book.

bear, the hunter who married a hare, and the man who went behind an iceberg and came back out as a seal. I touched the fur of my polar bear pants as I listened. We lived with, ate, and wore the skins of these animals. Jens's voice went soft and the words droned, putting us into a sweet trance. He said he sometimes dreamed about an animal that he would kill the next day, and in doing so, "ate his soul," the words translated literally. I didn't know if I would ever be able to sleep again without that voice and those stories. Maybe I would begin having those dreams too. Hours later, Mikele returned clutching two rabbits. "Ukaliqtuq," he caught a hare, Ilaitsuk said, turning to me. Even in the middle of the night she tried to teach me new words.

As she prepared to leave Greenland, Ehrlich wrote:

Soon it would be November, the month of unbroken night. The ice floor would be only weakly lighted when there was a moon. The Greenlandic word to denote this time of year is Tutsarfiq, meaning "one is listening," as if light were a divine presence whom we ask for mercy and tell our stories.

and

. . . darkness spread like cream over Greenland's humped-up back of ice. But nothing could diminish the population of spirits who still live on the glaciers, mountains, and beaches: sprites with no noses, giants traveling open water in half-kayaks, inland ice dwellers, naked spirits who steal hunters' seals, mountain dwarfs, and stones that are alive.

As black days came unnumbered, merging with night, the *pulaar*—visits between villagers—started up again. They told new stories about animal and human doings, about the demise of their traditional lifeways and melting ice caps, and waited, in their cold heaven, for the coming of light.

Part II

The Antarctic

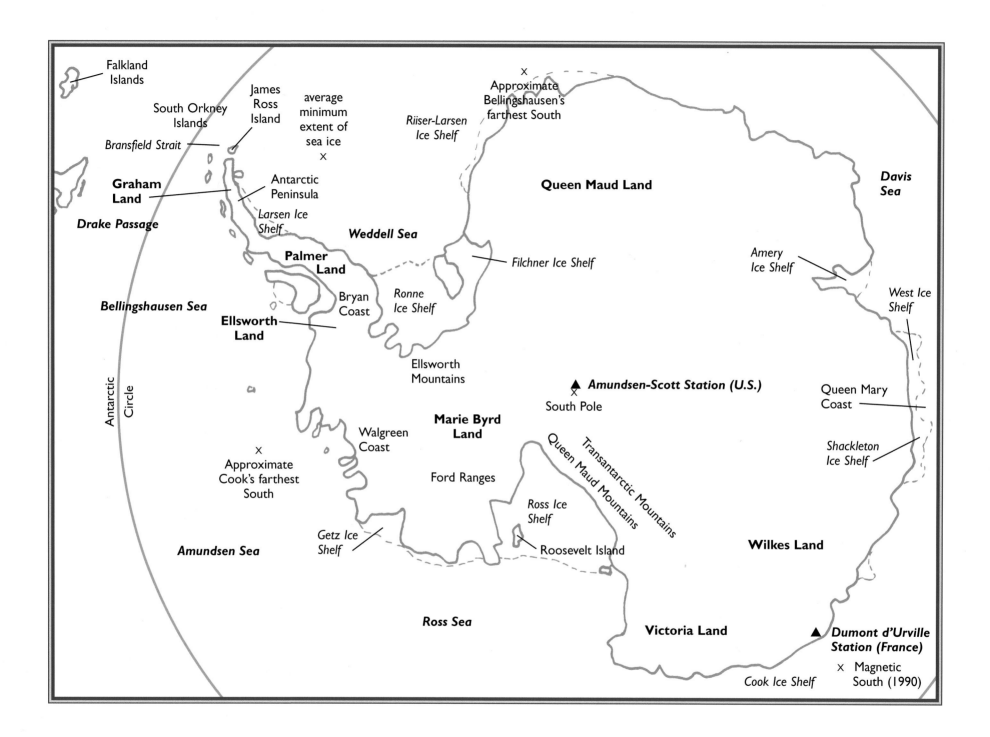

Falkland
Islands

South Orkney
Islands

James
Ross
Island

average
minimum
extent of
sea ice
×

Bransfield Strait

*Riiser-Larsen
Ice Shelf*

Approximate
Bellingshausen's
farthest South
×

*Davis
Sea*

**Graham
Land**

Antarctic
Peninsula

Queen Maud Land

Drake Passage

*Larsen Ice
Shelf*

Weddell Sea

**Palmer
Land**

Filchner Ice Shelf

*Amery
Ice Shelf*

Bellingshausen Sea

Bryan
Coast

*Ronne
Ice Shelf*

*West Ice
Shelf*

**Ellsworth
Land**

Ellsworth
Mountains

▲ **Amundsen-Scott Station (U.S.)**
×
South Pole

Queen Mary
Coast

Antarctic
Circle

×
Approximate
Cook's farthest
South

Walgreen
Coast

**Marie Byrd
Land**

Ford Ranges

Transantarctic Mountains

Queen Maud Mountains

*Shackleton
Ice Shelf*

Wilkes Land

*Getz Ice
Shelf*

Amundsen Sea

*Ross Ice
Shelf*

Roosevelt Island

Ross Sea

Victoria Land

▲ **Dumont d'Urville
Station (France)**

× Magnetic
South (1990)

Cook Ice Shelf

Antarctic Exploration Time Line

332 B.C.   Greek philosopher Aristotle writes that the landmass of the Arctic must be balanced by something at the other end of the Earth, and names it *Ant-Artic-a*

A.D. ~1000–1300s   Europeans believe that Antarctica has a lot of people, products for trade, and green pastures

~1272   Marco Polo explores China

~1325–early 1500s   Renaissance of arts and culture in Europe

1340s   "Black Death" plague first sweeps Europe

1492   Christopher Columbus explores West Indies and beyond to the New World

1498   Vasco da Gama rounds Africa to explore India

1498   Christopher Columbus explores South America

1513   Balboa explores the Pacific Ocean

1519–1522   Magellan circumnavigates the globe

Late 1570s   Francis Drake reaches 57 degrees south latitude

1575–1590s   Tycho Brahe sets up an astronomical observatory and develops his theory of a sun-centered solar system

1580   Francis Drake returns to England after circumnavigating the globe

1610   Galileo uses his telescope to discover Jupiter's moons

1772–1775   Captain James Cook gets within 100 miles of Antarctica

1776   Declaration of Independence is signed

1778   Captain James Cook explores Hawaii

1820   Thaddeus Bellingshausen, William Smith, Edward Bransfield, and Nathaniel Palmer all see different parts of Antarctica on their separate expeditions

1840   Charles Wilkes and Jules Sébastien César Dumont d'Urville discover more extensive areas of Antarctic coastline

1841   Sir James Clark Ross claims Antarctica for Queen Victoria of Britain

1849   California Gold Rush

1861–1865   U.S. Civil War

1895   Whaling boat captains Henryk Bull and Leonard Kristensen venture far into Antarctic waters to slay whales

1902 and 1904   Roald Amundsen and Robert Scott each attempt to reach the South Pole. Neither succeeds

1908   Ernest Shackleton leads an expedition to the South Pole, but doesn't reach it

1911 and 1912   Amundsen is the first man to reach the South Pole, in December 1911. Scott reaches it in early 1912, and dies on his way back

1914–1918   World War I

1929   Admiral Richard Byrd flies over the South Pole, accompanied by a Boy Scout

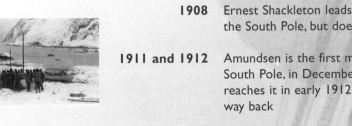

1938   Helicopters are first used in Antarctica for aerial photography

1939–1945   World War II

1950–1975   Vietnam War

1956   Antarctica tourism is launched

1957–1958   Antarctica becomes a science lab, with more than 60 international groups of scientists studying on the continent

1961   Antarctica Treaty signed by nations with claims to its territory; continent becomes jointly owned and managed

1962   John Glenn, Jr., becomes the first American to orbit the Earth

1980–1994   Bill Green studies Antarctic lakes

2000   Explorers Ann Bancroft and Liv Arnesen become the first women to cross Antarctica on skis

~   indicates approximate date

9

Captain James Cook's Three Voyages to Antarctica's Edges, 1768–1775

Antarctica lies at the bottom of the world. It's about 2,500 miles from Africa, 1,500 miles from Australia, and 450 miles from the tip of South America. It's much farther away from Europe than the Arctic is, and it has no native peoples. Antarctica is the coldest continent on the planet.

The History of Antarctica

Almost 600 million years ago, the ice world of Antarctica began to form close to the equator—much farther north than where it is now. It was a tropical land, full of plants and, later, animals.

Pancake ice is found throughout polar waters.

James Cook

Today you can find fossils of ancient ferns and even dinosaurs in Antarctica. But the land began to move south. When it moved over the South Pole, it quickly cooled. Animals and plants did not survive this change. Volcanoes and other mountains formed, and snow was compressed into icy glaciers. Ice now blankets 99 percent of Antarctica's surface, with almost all of the open land found in one area—the Antarctic Peninsula. The ice in Antarctica is thick and heavy. It is an average of 8,000 feet deep (that's about a mile and a half), and its weight presses the Trans-

Cold Waters

Deep underwater currents carry cold water away from Antarctica toward the rest of the world. It is estimated that these massive frigid rivers that flow within the ocean cool our planet's warmer oceans by a couple of degrees. A roughly circular cold zone, called the Southern Ocean, surrounds Antarctica at and inside 60 degrees south latitude.

antarctic Mountain Range, a 3,000-mile line of mountains, down nearly to sea level in many places. Ninety-one percent of all the ice in the world is found in Antarctica. Antarctica is immense—it's larger than the United States and Mexico put together. Its size and shape change with the seasons. Antarctica covers about 5.5 million square miles. Because a lot of ice is attached to its coasts, however, the total mass of land and ice can reach from 7 million square miles in the summer to 13 million square miles in the winter. The ice attached to Antarctica never melts, but large pieces (sometimes as big as the state of Rhode Island) break off and drift into the ocean. It's easy to see why early explorers such as James Cook found this sea ice impenetrable.

The Antarctic continent is also a dramatic desert. It only gets 4 to 20 inches of snowfall each year, and most of that falls near its coasts. Some places in the United States get hundreds of inches of snow in just one year! The coldest temperature ever recorded on Earth, −129.9° F (−90° C), was recorded in Antarctica.

As if this isn't enough to make people think twice about visiting there, the continent is surrounded by the Antarctic Convergence, a broad, fierce ocean current. Deathly cold water swirls out from the continent in all directions, where it encounters the warmer waters of the Atlantic, Pacific, and Indian oceans. The difference in temperature in this zone, both in the water and in the air, creates unending mists, fogs, and powerful storms that can reach the force of hurricanes. A ship requires a long time to cross the Antarctic Convergence before it encounters the dramatic white choke of sea ice that lies south of it.

Antarctica is a remote, cold, and vast world. In the early days, before anyone ever set foot there, people wondered about the continent and what might be found there. Some people thought that, because Antarctica was at the bottom of the world, people would have to walk on their heads, feet in the air, there. Others thought that people there would just fall off the bottom of the planet. Still others imagined Antarctica as a lush, green world filled with cheerful people. In 1870 a man named Jules Verne wrote a story about a group of people who travel to the South Pole. The book is called *Twenty Thousand Leagues Under the Sea*. Here is how the author imagined Antarctica:

> About eight o'clock in the morning of the 16th of March the *Nautilus*, following the fifty-fifth meridian, cut the antarctic polar circle. Ice surrounded us on all sides, and closed the horizon. But Captain Nemo went from one opening to another, still going higher. I cannot express my astonishment at the beauties of these new regions. The ice took most surprising forms. Here the grouping formed an oriental town, with innumerable mosques and minarets; there a fallen city thrown to the earth, as it were, by some convulsion of nature. The whole aspect was constantly changed by the oblique rays of the sun, or lost in the greyish fog amidst hurricanes of snow. Detonations and falls were heard on all sides, great overthrows of icebergs, which altered the whole landscape like a diorama. Often seeing no exit, I thought we were definitely prisoners; but instinct guiding him at the slightest indication, Captain Nemo would discover a new pass . . .

Exploration of Antarctica Begins

During Europe's Age of Discovery, explorers rushed in all directions to find "new" lands. Magellan saw Tierra del Fuego in South America, and by the late 1570s Francis Drake reached 57 degrees south latitude, the farthest south yet reached, as he sailed around the world. In 1719, a British sea captain named George Shelvocke was forced south in a storm off South America and saw an iceberg. But none of these explorers even caught a glimpse of the continent of Antarctica.

Yet people still believed that Antarctica existed, and they were still hungry to claim new lands. The British Admiralty decided to send an accomplished seafarer, Captain James Cook (1728–1779), in search of the continent. Cook had already explored parts of the subarctic and of the South Pacific, and he was given very specific instructions on which route to take and at what latitudes to seek Antarctica. He was also told how to treat the people who were imagined to live in Antarctica. In his book, *Voyage Toward the South Pole*, Cook wrote:

> I was also directed to observe the genius, temper, disposition, and number, of the inhabitants, if there were any, and endeavour, by all proper means, to cultivate a friendship and alliance with them; making them presents of such things as they might value; inviting them to traffic, and shewing them every kind of civility and regard.

Cook set sail on his ship, the *Endeavor*, in August 1768 with a crew of 94 people, including several scientists, in a ship filled with sheep, pigs, ducks, chickens, and a goat. Just as he had been told to do, he sailed past Tierra del Fuego, went on to Tahiti, and then traveled to 40 degrees south latitude in pursuit of his goal: to claim Antarctica for England. But he did not find Antarctica. He was looking in the wrong place!

The voyage was not a total failure. Cook explored and mapped vast areas of New Zealand's coast, which had recently been discovered by the Dutch. He explored the areas between New Zealand and Australia and between Australia and New Guinea. He claimed many islands there for England and mapped the Great Barrier Reef. He also brought back hundreds of plants that had never before been seen in Europe, as well as information about the *aborigines*, the natives of the land. When his ship returned to England in 1771, Cook became very famous for his many discoveries.

Captain James Cook Steps to the Forefront of Antarctic Exploration

Cook still wanted to find Antarctica, which he thought was farther south than he had been allowed to go during his first voyage. The British government agreed to let him try again. This time he was given two ships for his voyage—the *Resolution* and the *Adventure*. Cook was told to

Penguins

Penguins are very interesting birds. They look like they're dressed up in tuxedos! They can swim like seals, waddle like ducks, and honk like geese. Penguins do not live in the Arctic at all, but Antarctica is home to seven different kinds: emperors, chinstraps, macaronis, gentoos, rockhoppers, kings, and adelies.

Penguins are superbly adapted to the frigid climate. Overlapping water-resistant feathers cover a layer of wooly down, which helps to keep them warm. Under their skin is a layer of fat, which also helps block out the cold. Penguins keep their eggs and babies warm by tucking them between their flippers and a roll of warm feathers. Parents alternate between keeping their young warm and fishing for food in the ocean. They cannot fly. Instead, they slide on their stomachs from the ice into the sea. Then they swim underwater, using their wings and feet as fins, and catch fish. Standing over three feet tall, the emperor is the largest of the penguins, and probably the hardiest. It lays its eggs on the Antarctic ice—in winter, when temperatures can easily drop to –70° F (–57° C). It helps that emperors are very social and huddle together against the cold, but their feats of egg-hatching and chick-rearing still remain

Portrait of James Cook, from his book *Voyage Toward the South Pole*.

amazing. Most emperor penguins breed on shelves of ice that jut out into the sea. They flock to their *rookeries* (bird nurseries) in the fall, and the females lay eggs from early May through June. The females, thin from weight lost during courtship and egg-laying, then return to feed at sea, leaving the male to keep the eggs warm by sitting on them.

take a route that extended as far south as he could go from New Zealand. When he had done that, he would sail around the Earth at 60 degrees south latitude. He left in 1772. In addition to his crew, the ships carried scientists, musicians, livestock, and the latest in equipment, including four chronometers to measure latitude.

On this second voyage, Cook became the first explorer to cross the Antarctic Circle. He and his men saw many penguins there. One crewmember even honked at them like a goose and got them to come close to the ship.

Cook and his crew were soon prevented from further exploration by fierce storms and icebergs. At one point he was only 80 miles from Antarctica, but he didn't know it. The fog and other weather conditions prevented Cook from seeing the land.

Returning north to New Zealand, Cook set out again in December 1773. His ship was well stocked with plenty of food, including sauerkraut and boiled pea pudding. In an effort to prevent scurvy among his men, Cook ordered them to eat fresh food in every port along the way.

In January 1774 Cook reached 70 degrees south latitude, farther south than any explorer had ventured. Yet there was still no sign of real land. Instead, he saw mirages and impassable sea ice.

How Long Does It Take to Freeze?

Explorers used Antarctica as a giant freezer. All that ice and cold made it very easy to keep their food from rotting. But different foods take different amounts of time to freeze, and some foods taste pretty bad once they've been frozen and then thawed. How long do you think it takes an egg to freeze? How about a glass of milk? You don't have to live in the Antarctic to find out—you can test this right at home in your freezer. This activity uses foods that the explorers brought along on their trips. They got their eggs from live chickens they brought with them.

1. Carefully crack the egg into one of the glasses or cups, being careful not to break the egg yolk.
2. Place the bread on the plate.
3. Pour the milk into the remaining glass or cup.
4. All of the foods, in their containers, should be about the same thickness or depth. Since the goal of this activity is to see which freezes first

Materials	
Adult supervision required	(about $1/2$-inch thick)
1 raw egg	Small freezer-safe
2 small freezer-safe glasses or cups	plate
1 piece of bread	$1/2$ cup milk
	Frying pan

and which takes the longest to freeze, it's important to make things as even as possible. (For example, two separate cups of milk will take an equal amount of time to freeze. But what if you compared a cup of milk to, say, a whole gallon? The gallon of milk would take much longer to freeze!)

5. Place all three containers in the freezer. Make sure that the containers aren't touching each other or other foods that are already in the freezer.
6. Wait 30 minutes, then check to see if they've frozen. Do this by gently poking each one with your finger. Do this carefully so that you don't end up dividing the food into two parts, since then your freezable amounts will be smaller. Have any of them frozen yet?

7. Keep freezing the foods and checking on them every 30 minutes. When a food completely freezes, remove it from the freezer and note how long it took to freeze. (It may be a couple of hours or more before all of the foods freeze.)
8. Which food froze first? Which took the longest to freeze? Can you figure out why?
9. Now let each food thaw just enough so that you can bite into the bread and drink some of the milk. (Do not taste the raw egg.) Taste the bread. Does it taste good or bad? How about the milk? Ask an adult to cook the egg for you in a frying pan. When it's cooked, taste it. How do you like it?
12. Based on your taste test, which food would be the best to take to Antarctica?

Note: To learn why these foods freeze at different rates and why some foods taste better than others after they've been frozen, check out the answers in the Selected Answers section in the back of the book.

Icebergs can float far from land.

During their journey Cook wrote in his journal:

The Clowds near the horizon were of a perfect Snow whiteness and were difficult to be distinguished from the Ice hills whose lofty summits reached the Clowds. The outer or Northern edge of this immence Ice field was composed of loose or broken ice so close packed together that nothing could enter it; about a Mile in began the firm ice, in one compact solid boddy and seemed to increase in height as you traced it to the South; In this field we counted Ninety Seven Ice Hills or Mountains, many of them vastly large. It was indeed my opinion as well as the opinion of most on board, that this Ice extended quite to the Pole or perhaps joins to some land, to which it had been wholy covered with Ice.

Albatrosses fly thousands of miles (kilometers) each year.

In 1775 Cook headed home, disappointed that he still had not found Antarctica. In his report, Cook said that maybe Antarctica did not really exist at all—at least, not the tropical paradise that many people thought Antarctica to be. "That there may be a continent or large tract of land near the Pole I would not deny," he wrote. "On the contrary I am of the opinion that there is, and it is probable that we have seen a part of it." But he believed that no ship would be able to reach it through the dangerous weather of the region and impenetrable ice.

Although Cook did not look for Antarctica again, this was not the last of his explorations. In 1779 he attempted to find the western entrance to the Northwest Passage. Instead he discovered a group of islands that he named the Sandwich Islands in honor of the Earl of Sandwich, one of the Englishmen who helped to finance his trip. After journeying to Alaska, Cook returned to the Sandwich Islands. Some of the local natives stole one of the small boats he had, and Cook tried to take the local chief hostage in order to get his boat back. Instead, he was stabbed to death on February 14, 1779.

Years later, the Sandwich Islands were renamed. They are now known as Hawaii.

Expeditions to find Antarctica waned, but commerce in the recently discovered lands and waters increased. By 1880 ships traveled to these areas in search of the multitudes of seals that Cook had described. The men who made these journeys captured and killed thousands and thousands of seals, and many of the men became very wealthy from selling the seals' furry pelts. In fact the first man to set foot on the continent of Antarctica was not an explorer, but a seal hunter.

This is called a *tabular* iceberg.

Celebrate Snow with Poems and an All-White Collage

Antarctic explorers were often amazed at the beauty of this vast, glittering icy world, and their journals reflect the awe they felt at seeing this amazing place of snow. You can celebrate the beauty of snow by writing a poem and creating an all-white collage.

1. First, write a poem that celebrates snow. You might want to think about a particular thing, such as a snowy tree or a dog playing in the snow, and make that the focus of your poem.

2. Try to remember the last time you were outside in the cold. How did you feel? What were you thinking? Where were you? Was it quiet or noisy outside? Were you in a beautiful place? If you could be anywhere snowy that you wanted, where would it be? What would it feel like? Maybe you'd like to be skiing down a mountain, or walking through the woods. Maybe you'd like to be watching penguins in Antarctica. Close your eyes and try to picture how it would be.

3. Now it's time to write your poem. Try to make your words give people the feeling of really being where you imagine you are, or really seeing the snowy scene you imagine in your head. Here are some of the tricks that poets use to help get across their ideas and feelings. You can write one poem or several

---

Materials

Adult supervision required

Pictures of Antarctica or another snowy place (use books for reference, or find a Web site, such as www.cool antarctica.com, that has pictures of these things)

Paper

Pen

Colored markers

Scissors

Assorted white objects such as cotton balls, bits of white fabric and paper, and white ornaments

1 piece of white poster board (whatever size you want your collage to be)

Glue

---

separate poems to try your hand at each of these tricks.

Use *sensory words*. These are words that involve your body's senses—smell, sight, hearing, taste, and touch. Describe a scene that gets people to think about their senses. How does your snowy scene smell? What does the air taste like? What do you see? What do you hear? Can you feel the cold on your nose?

Be creative with your words. Instead of just saying "snowflakes are cold," you might say something like "the snowflakes fell on my eyelids like frozen kisses."

Create a list of words that describe the snow experience. Suppose you choose a snowball as your subject. Write down all the things you can think of that could be done with that snowball. For example, you could throw it. You could eat it. You could roll it down a hill. You could stuff it down your friend's shirt as a joke. What else could be done with that snowball? The things you come up with will help you write your poem.

Try using words that rhyme. This is often the poetic form that people think of first. Here's an example: "A snowball is cool/it's a white jewel."

Have fun writing your poem! You can write as many as you want. Don't forget to give each one a title.

4. Now, make an all-white collage to celebrate snow. Neatly rewrite your finished poem or poems onto the poster board. Space them out so that you can add decorations around each poem to frame it.

5. Select white items that suggest the theme of each poem, such as cotton balls for falling snow, and glue them around your poem. Let you imagination and creativity soar!

6. You can use your collage to decorate your room, or perhaps to give as a gift to a friend or to your mom or dad. Be sure to sign your name to it, and write the date you made it on the board as well.

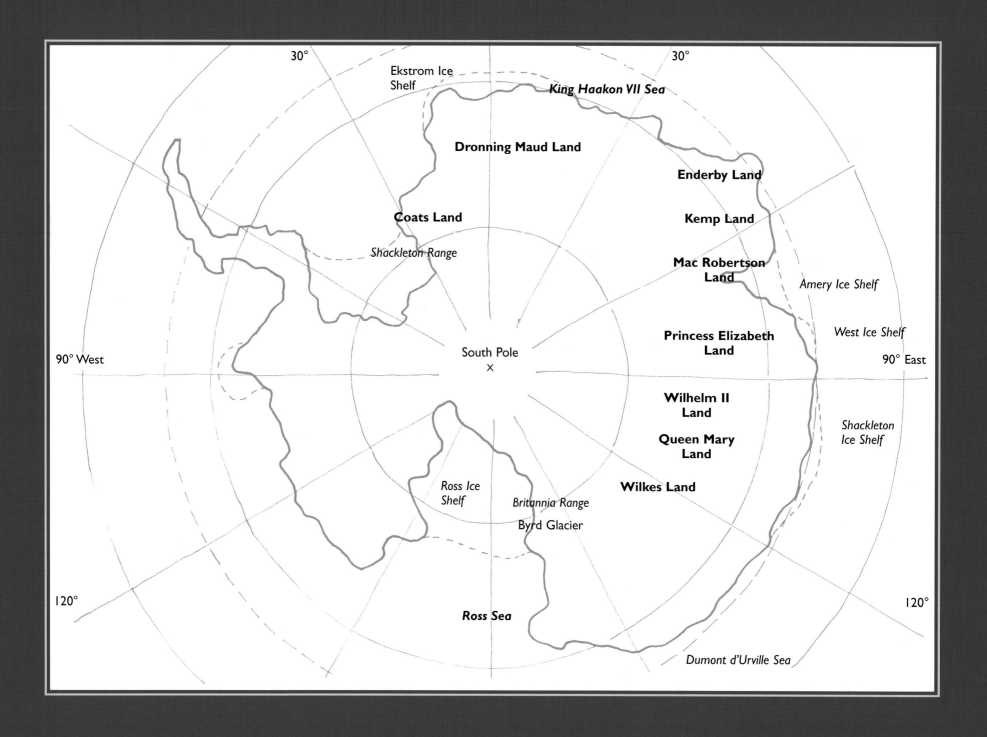

10

James Clark Ross Explores Antarctica by Ship, 1839–1843

After James Cook's voyages, most people became convinced that the extreme southern ocean was truly treacherous, and that any land discovered there would not be inhabited by people, or even have good resources, such as oil, that could be used and sold.

A few adventurers still wanted to be the first to find Antarctica, however—that is, if it existed at all. People still weren't sure!

The first explorers to see the Antarctic land were not certain that they had actually found a new continent. In 1820 the Russian explorer Thaddeus von Bellingshausen spotted it, and just three days later William Smith, the captain of a British cargo ship, also saw the land. Americans Nathaniel Palmer and Edward Bransfield saw

A bird's-eye view of Antarctica.

the Antarctic Peninsula, the most northwestern area of Antarctica, in 1820 as well. But none of these men were sure that what they saw was a continent. They thought the land might be just another island, and they did not have time to try and circumnavigate it (sail all the way around it) to find out. Antarctic summers were usually far too short for explorers to attempt something like that.

By the 1830s several more seal hunters and explorers had sighted different areas of the Antarctic coast. French explorer Jules Sébastien César Dumont d'Urville even took a few penguins back to his country to prove he'd been to Antarctica. Usually, whenever someone spotted land—whether it was an island or part of the Antarctic continent—he claimed it for his country. In 1840 Charles Wilkes, a United States Navy lieutenant, landed on the coast. He looked around and decided that he saw enough territory in the distance to know that he was *not* on an island. Even though he didn't prove it, Wilkes was the first person to officially claim that Antarctica was indeed a continent.

James Clark Ross Sets His Sights on Antarctica

Meanwhile, James Clark Ross (1800–1862) was exploring areas of the Arctic. Ross was an experienced and successful explorer: in 1831 he and

his uncle, John Ross, discovered the Magnetic North Pole. By the late 1830s, Ross set his sights on the other end of the world, Antarctica. He wanted to be the first to sail through the pack ice and reach farthest south. Over the next several seasons, Ross explored the Antarctic wilderness, and he traveled about as far south as possible by ocean: about 78 degrees south latitude, along the edge of a large ice shelf on Antarctica's south side. This mass of ice was later named the Ross Ice Shelf in honor of James Ross.

On his ships, the *Erebus* and the *Terror*, the same two ships later lost with Frankin's expedition, Ross explored the edge of the massive ice shelf by sea. The Ross Ice Shelf's edge is a cliff of ice that several stories high. It extends for about 400 miles where it meets the sea and stretches about 600 miles inland. The largest of Antarctica's ice shelves, it is approximately the size of France. Extending from the land out into the sea, ice shelves such as this one rise and fall with the tides. They can grow in size, stretching farther out into the ocean some years than others. Though Ross could not land, he explored the ice shelf over two separate summers on his voyage, claiming large stretches of Antarctica for Britain in the process. Ross was awed by what he saw and wrote about it in his book *A Voyage of Discovery and Research in the Southern and Antarctic Regions*:

It was a beautiful clear evening, and we had a most enchanting view of the two magnificent

Sir James Clark Ross.

ranges of mountains, whose lofty peaks, perfectly covered with eternal snow, rose to elevations varying from seven to ten thousand feet above the level of the ocean. The glaciers that filled their intervening valleys, and which descended from near the mountain summits, projected in many places several miles into the sea, and terminated in lofty perpendicular cliffs. In a few places the rocks broke through

How Glaciers Form

Every glacier begins as a field of fallen snow. Over hundreds of years, more snow falls onto the original snow or is swept into the area by wind. The snow gradually compacts, and, as the snow crystals lose their edges and become rounded, they compact further. Finally, no visible air spaces remain among the grains of snow: the mass has become ice. More than 95 percent of Antarctica's ice is in the form of glaciers.

their icy covering, by which alone we could be assured that land formed the nucleus of this, to appearance, enormous iceberg.

Ross keenly wanted to find the Magnetic South Pole. Not only would it be a huge scientific achievement, but it would mean that he could claim to be the person who found *both* magnetic poles! Ross also wanted to claim more lands for Britain, so he headed east to look for both. Breaking through pack ice, he entered what is now called the Ross Sea. (This is the area of Antarctic where Ross Island and the United States' scientific base McMurdo Station is located. You can read about this McMurdo Station in Chapter 15.)

Although Ross did travel farther south than any other explorer had, he did not land and so was not able to approach the Magnetic South Pole, which lay some 160 miles inland. (Like the Magnetic North Pole, the location of the Magnetic South Pole moves around.) He was, however, the first person to see a volcano in Antarctica, in 1841—and it was erupting! Now named Mt. Erebus, the volcano is an island in the Ross Sea. As he wrote in his book:

The discovery of an active volcano in so high a southern latitude cannot but be esteemed a circumstance of high geological importance and interest, and contribute to throw some further light on the physical construction of our globe . . . At 4 P.M. Mount Erebus was observed to emit smoke and flame in unusual quantities, producing a most grand spectacle. A volume of dense smoke was projected at each successive jet with great force, in a vertical column, to the height of between fifteen hundred and two thousand feet above the mouth of the crater, when condensing first at its upper part, it descended in mist or snow, and gradually dispersed, to be succeeded by another splendid exhibition of the same kind in about half an hour afterwards, although the intervals between the eruptions were by no means regular. The diameter of the columns of smoke was between two and three hundred feet, as near as we could

measure it; whenever the smoke cleared away, the bright red flame that filled the mouth of the crater was clearly perceptible; and some of the officers believed they could see streams of lava pouring down its sides until lost beneath the snow which descended from a few hundred feet below the crater, and projected its perpendicular icy cliff several miles into the ocean. Mount Terror was much more free from snow, especially on its eastern side . . ."

The most southerly active volcano in the world, Mt. Erebus has erupted just a few times since Ross saw it spewing fiery red lava onto its bright white ice and snow slopes. Over 12,000 feet high, it is one of only two active volcanoes in all of Antarctica. (The other one is called Deception Island.) Mt. Erebus is located at the end of the Transantarctic Mountain Chain, which extends for approximately 3,000 miles. Most of these mountains were once also active volcanoes, but they are now considered extinct.

Ross saw many whales during his voyage in the Antarctic. The whales had never encountered humans before, and were not afraid of them. They often came very close to the ships to stare at the sailors. As Ross wrote in his book:

We continued our course to the southward, amongst numerous icebergs and much drift ice. A great many whales were seen, chiefly of

Explorers do not sail into ice caves like these!

Antarctic Fish

Just 120 species of fish live in Antarctica's waters, a very small proportion of the more than 20,000 species of fish swimming through the waters of the world. Many of these polar fish have a substance like a natural antifreeze that circulates through their bodies, preventing them from freezing solid in the icy waters. Some have blood that is almost transparent. Another, called the deep-water dragon fish, has a face that looks like a dragon's. And yet another, called the rattail, has a tail that looks like a rat's!

Baby fur seals.

the common black kind, greatly resembling, but said to be distinct from, the Greenland whale: sperm, as well as hunchbacked whales, were also observed; of the common black species we might have killed any number we pleased: they appeared chiefly to be of unusually large size, and would doubtless yield a great quantity of oil, and were so tame that our ships sailing close past did not seem to disturb them. During a short period of calm in the afternoon many marine invertebrata were taken, amongst them the Clio borealis and beautiful little Argonauta arctica, upon which, doubtless, the whales were feeding, as it is well known that these creatures constitute the whale's food in the northern seas.

Toward the end of his journey, Ross tried to circumnavigate Antarctica, beginning along the western side of the Antarctic Peninsula. In the process he claimed some more islands for Britain, but pack ice and bad weather prevented him from going further south along the coast.

When he returned home, Ross was offered the chance to lead another expedition to the

Make a Barometer

Polar explorers used barometers to find out when storms were approaching. A *barometer* is a device that measures air pressure (also called barometric pressure). It measures the weight of air, which changes as weather conditions change. Simple barometers have been used for centuries. Some of the earliest barometers, called "storm glasses," used water to measure air pressure. You can make your own barometer to keep track of changing weather conditions.

1. Put the ruler in the glass or jar. Place it in so that the 1-inch mark on the ruler is at the bottom and facing out toward you, so you can see the measurements. Tape the upper part of the ruler to the inside of the top of the glass or jar. (Tape only the upper part of the ruler.)
2. Tape the upper part of the straw to the inside of the glass, next to the ruler and about ½ inch from the bottom of the glass or jar. (Tape only the upper part of the straw.)
3. Pour 2 inches of water into the glass or jar. Use the ruler to measure your water.
4. Chew the gum for about 3 minutes.
5. Put the gum in your hand and hold your hand very near your mouth. Now, suck on the straw

Materials

Ruler	Clear tape
Clear, clean water glass or empty food jar (the size doesn't matter, but the mouth of the glass or jar—the part that's open at the top—must be at least a couple of inches wide)	Clear plastic straw with a bendable section
	1 piece of gum (either regular gum or bubble gum)
	Pen
	1 11 × 17-inch piece of paper

until the water in the straw reaches the 3½ inch mark on the ruler. Quickly—*very quickly*—stuff the gum over and around the top of the straw to seal it off. Make sure that the water level in the straw is between the 3-inch and the 4-inch mark. The less air that's trapped in the straw, the better your barometer will work. (You can do this step over again if you need to.) That's it—you've made your very own barometer! Now, how do you use it?

6. With your pen and paper, make a chart where you can fill in four notations every day for at least two weeks: the day's date, the water measurement level in the straw, the weather (fair, rainy, windy), and the barometric pressure that day as recorded by a nearby weather bureau. (Look online, call a local television station, or watch the Weather Channel on cable television to get the phone number of your local weather bureau.)
7. Every day for two weeks, record the day's information in your chart. Try to collect your information at about the same time every day. If you think a storm is coming, record your information every 4 to 6 hours if you can.
8. After several days of recording information, you may be able to spot some trends. For one thing, the higher the barometric pressure (according to the weather bureau or other source), the lower the water level in the straw, and vice versa. This is because the greater pressure of

the air pushes the water down and it finds its only "escape" by moving up the straw—there, less air is pressing on it because you sucked out a lot of the air from the straw and sealed it before the air could move back in. A "high" barometric pressure in the United States is about 30.50. A low one is about 29.50, and our average barometric pressure is about 29.90.

9. At the end of the two weeks, take a look at the information you collected and see if you can tell how your barometer indicates weather changes. How many of the following did you spot?

- Water level in the straw lowers:
  This happens as the barometric pressure falls. A steady fall in barometric pressure is a sign that bad weather is on its way.
- Water level in the straw rises:
  Unless it happens very quickly, this indicates that the barometric pressure is steadily increasing—a sign that the weather isn't changing very much.
- Water level in the straw does not change:
  This happens when there is no change in the barometric pressure, and it means that the weather is clear and will stay clear.
- Water level in the straw changes very quickly (either up or down):
  Look out—a storm is coming! (The amount of the change is not as important as the speed of the change.)

Arctic. He declined. The offer was accepted by John Franklin—and you remember what happened to him! (To refresh your memory, see Chapter 5.)

The Antarctic lay quiet for more than 50 years after Ross's departure. The United States, which had its hands full with the Civil War, temporarily stopped exploring the Antarctic, as did other countries. Even the seal hunters left, after wiping out a large percentage of the seal population—there weren't enough seals around to kill anymore. Finally, in the mid-1890s, people began to come to Antarctica again. Henryk Bull, the captain of a whale-hunting ship, visited Antarctica, and, in 1899, a group of whalers led by the Norwegian Carsten Borchgrevink arrived as well. Two of the men who took care of the dogs on the Borchgrevink's ship were the first people to actually spend the night on Antarctica, and the whole group was, by most accounts, the first to overwinter there. During this period, just one scientific expedition ship, Britain's *Challenger*, explored the region.

But Antarctic exploration was about to increase. From 1901 to 1922, the world witnessed what was called the "heroic age" of Antarctic exploration.

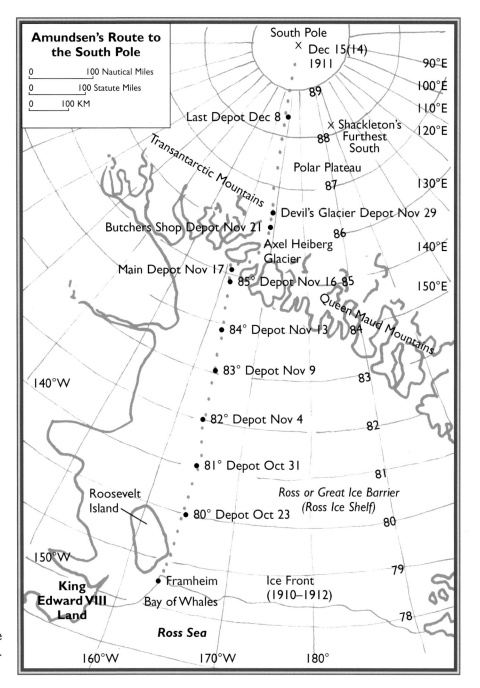

Amundsen's Route to the South Pole

0	100 Nautical Miles
0	100 Statute Miles
0	100 KM

South Pole
✗ Dec 15(14)
1911

90°E
100°E
89
110°E

Last Depot Dec 8 •
✗ Shackleton's
88 Furthest
South
120°E

Polar Plateau
87
130°E

• Devil's Glacier Depot Nov 29

Butchers Shop Depot Nov 21 •
86
140°E

Axel Heiberg
Glacier

Main Depot Nov 17 •
• 85° Depot Nov 16 85
150°E

Transantarctic Mountains

Queen Maud Mountains

• 84° Depot Nov 13 84

• 83° Depot Nov 9
83

140°W

• 82° Depot Nov 4
82

• 81° Depot Oct 31
81

Roosevelt
Island

*Ross or Great Ice Barrier
(Ross Ice Shelf)*

• 80° Depot Oct 23
80

150°W

79

• Framheim
**King
Edward VIII
Land**
Bay of Whales

Ice Front
(1910–1912)

78

Ross Sea

160°W   170°W   180°

Roald Amundsen's route
to the South Pole.

Roald Amundsen in 1909.

Every country wanted to lay claim to as much of Antarctica's land as possible. British explorer Robert Scott's first trip to Antarctica sparked a sense of competition among the countries. That spirit of competition exploded as Scott set out for Antarctica a second time. It would be his most famous journey ever.

Robert Falcon Scott (1868–1912) was a British naval officer who had originally been

Robert Falcon Scott before his final South Pole effort.

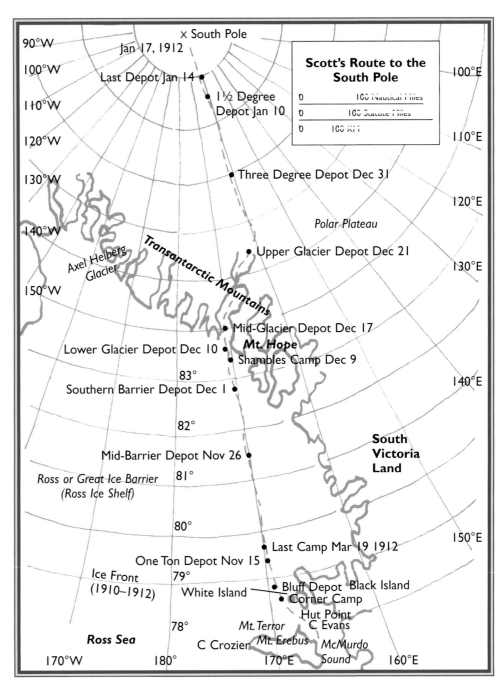

Scott's Route to the
South Pole

0 ___ 100 Nautical Miles
0 ___ 100 Statute Miles
0 ___ 100 KM

x South Pole
Jan 17, 1912
Last Depot Jan 14 •
• 1½ Degree
Depot Jan 10

• Three Degree Depot Dec 31

Polar Plateau

• Upper Glacier Depot Dec 21

Axel Helberg Glacier

Transantarctic Mountains

• Mid-Glacier Depot Dec 17
Mt. Hope
Lower Glacier Depot Dec 10 •
• Shambles Camp Dec 9

83°
Southern Barrier Depot Dec 1 •

82°

**South
Victoria
Land**

Mid-Barrier Depot Nov 26 •

Ross or Great Ice Barrier 81°
(Ross Ice Shelf)

80°

Last Camp Mar 19 1912

One Ton Depot Nov 15 •

Ice Front 79°
(1910–1912)
White Island

Bluff Depot Black Island
Corner Camp

Hut Point
C Evans
78° Mt. Terror
Ross Sea Mt. Erebus McMurdo
C Crozier Sound

170°W   180°   170°E   160°E

90°W   100°E
100°W
110°W   110°E
120°W
130°W   120°E
140°W   130°E
150°W   140°E
150°E

trained as a torpedo specialist (considered a high-tech weapon in those days). He came to the attention of the Royal Geographic Society, which wanted to revive Antarctic exploration. The society convinced the navy to send Scott on an expedition to Antarctica.

Scott's first Antarctic voyage lasted from 1901 to 1904. He was accompanied during part of the expedition by a man who would later

Robert Scott's
route to the
South Pole.

become one of the most famous explorers in history—Ernest Shackleton (see Chapter 12). During this first trip, Scott discovered a new area of the continent, which he named King Edward VII Land, and he was the first person to observe a penguin rookery (a breeding colony with thousands of nesting birds). After overwintering at McMurdo Sound, Scott ventured farther south than any previous explorer: 82 degrees 17 minutes south latitude. He wrote a book about the trip, called *The Voyage of* Discovery (*Discovery* was the name of his ship). Published in 1905, it was a tremendous success. He became famous for his discipline (both his self-discipline and the discipline with which he managed his crew), his inability to prevent scurvy among his crew, and his preference for "man-hauling" the sledges (sleds), using men instead of dog teams to pull them.

Roald Amundsen (1872–1928) had an even more illustrious history of polar achievements before he and Scott began their race to the South Pole. Amundsen was the first to sail the Northwest Passage through the Arctic and the first to prove that the Magnetic North Pole moved around. He had hoped to be the first to reach the Geographic North Pole, but was disappointed when both Cook and Peary announced that they had made it there. As a native of snowy Norway, he was an expert skier and outdoorsman. He taught himself how to make an igloo, coat the runners of sledges with

Make Pemmican

Amundsen took pemmican along to Antarctica because it is a high-energy food that lasts a long time when the weather is cold. It was invented by the American Indians but was also used by Europeans (and others) in the early 20th century.

1. Preheat the oven to 200° F (93° C).
2. Place the meat strips in a single layer in the roasting pan (do not grease the pan first). Leave as much space as possible between the strips.
3. Place the pan in the heated oven. Cook for about 2½ hours, until the meat almost feels like dry leather, but will still bend without breaking. Remove the pan, turn off the oven, and let the meat cool.
4. Cut and mash the cooled meat into tiny pieces, almost to a powder. The closer you get it to a powder, the better the pemmican will hold together at the end. Place the powdered meat in a medium-sized bowl and set it aside.
5. Melt the butter or suet in a small saucepan over very low heat. Don't let it boil or brown.
6. Pour the melted butter into a small bowl.
7. Add the mixture to the bowl with the powdered

Materials	
Adult supervision required	Medium-sized bowl
4 strips of raw beef, each about 4 inches long and 1 inch wide, after any fat has been trimmed off and discarded (flank, round, or strip steak is best)	5–6 tablespoons of butter or suet (animal fat)
	Small saucepan
	Mesh strainer
	Small bowl
	2–4 tablespoons of granola, dried berries, and raisins
Roasting pan	4 small plastic bags

beef and mix together thoroughly. Roll the mixture into four balls about the size of golf balls. Place them in the refrigerator and chill for at least an hour, until the butter has solidified and will hold the mixture together.
8. Place each pemmican ball into a plastic bag. Partially seal the bags shut, leaving a small opening so that the balls will dry out a bit. Store in the refrigerator overnight.
9. When the pemmican balls have dried, they are ready to eat. Pemmican balls may be stored in the refrigerator for up to a month.

frozen moss, and wear reindeer and sealskin fur clothing—all practices that he learned from reading about native Arctic people and from seeing them firsthand. He carried an "Eskimo dictionary" with him in the Arctic so that he could speak with the natives and learn as much as he could from them. Amundsen was known for being a democratic leader, but he also had a

Amundsen, before his South Pole trip, researched the meat his men would need to preserve their strength.

reputation for having difficulty raising funds for his voyages. He asked the Armour Meatpacking Company in the United States for free *pemmican* (dried meat that is pounded flat and mixed with beef fat) for a trip. He often got some of the money for his trips by agreeing to tell his story to certain newspapers in exchange for money. Amundsen was the protégé of fellow Norwegian Fridtjof Nansen (see Chapter 6), who at this point was incredibly famous. Nansen offered to help Amundsen raise money for his next voyage. He even let him use the *Fram*, the ship that had carried Nansen farthest north in his era. Amundsen had the ship retrofitted from a sailing ship with a steam engine to a sailing ship with a diesel engine. This improved the ship's power and safety.

Scott and Amundsen Prepare for Their Journeys

When Robert Scott announced his plan to be first to the South Pole, Amundsen decided to race him to it. He kept this a secret, though, and continued to raise funds for a voyage to the *North* Pole. All along he had been telling people that he was going to the North Pole, and he was afraid that people would not give him money if he told them he'd changed his plans. Amundsen wanted the race to be fair, and he decided that Scott was entitled to the route out of McMurdo Sound, since he had explored there during his previous Antarctic voyage. Amundsen chose the Bay of Whales in the Ross Ice Shelf as his own launch point for the race. (Look at the map to follow the route.) It was closer to the South Pole, but the route would lead over entirely unknown terrain for much of his expedition.

Though Scott knew nothing of Amundsen's plan, he needed to rush through preparations for his voyage because German and French explorers were also arranging for a departure to Antarctica. It was South Pole mania! He didn't have time to train his men to ski well and he failed to select the best dogs. Scott decided to bring along ponies as well as dogs for transportation. In addition, he chose to bring "motorized sledges," which had never been tested in such extreme conditions. Equipped with all of these things, Scott raced off from the British coast on June 1, 1910, amid the cheers of thousands of his fellow citizens.

Amundsen planned his voyage more carefully. He selected a smaller group of men (19 men, compared to Scott's 65) to train and bring along, and he read all the books he could find about Antarctica. He bought the best dogs (from Greenland) and trained them well, designing their harnesses the way the native Arctic people did. He launched his expedition from Norway—and he didn't tell his men they were going to the *South* Pole instead of the North Pole until they were far from home and any other area where they could notify someone. He did, however give them all the chance to leave the expedition and return home. Everyone decided to stay.

Both men knew that being the first to let the rest of the world know he'd made it to the South Pole was almost as important as actually *being* the first to reach the South Pole. Neither Amundsen nor Scott trusted the very newest invention for communicating, the wireless radio, and each planned to notify the world that he'd reached the South Pole by cable. Amundsen planned to send his message from the island of Tasmania (part of Australia), and Scott intended to do so from New Zealand. There was certainly no place in Antarctica from which to send a cable.

The Race Begins

The race was underway—although Scott didn't know that it was a race at all. He sailed as far as Australia before he received this telegram: "Beg leave to inform you *Fram* proceeding Antarctic Amundsen." Scott was very surprised! Exactly 10 days later, on January 14, 1911, Amundsen landed in the Bay of Whales. Scott had already reached McMurdo Sound. The sprint to the South Pole was on.

But first, both groups needed to settle into their base huts, where they would test all their equipment and make multiple trips inland to drop off extra supplies at various points, called *depots*, along their designated routes. Not only did this allow them to carry fewer supplies along the journey, it also gave them a measure of safety—if the supplies they did have with them were somehow lost or destroyed, there would be more waiting for the men up ahead. Amundsen marked his depots with black flags and dog food—hoping that the dogs' sense of smell would help them find the buried supplies later.

Antarctic Birds

Millions of birds fly over and fish in the Antarctic waters during the summer months. The wandering albatross, the prion, and the skua are three interesting examples.

The wandering albatross is a huge white bird with wings tipped in brown. It has more wing feathers than any other bird on earth. Landing only to nest, it soars over the ocean for most of its exceptionally long life of 80–85 years. It dives into the ocean for fish, then spits out excess saltwater through two nostrils on its beak. The female albatross does not become a parent until it is between 10 and 14 years old—much older than the average bird. An albatross chick is a big bird, and it takes almost a year to fully develop. For this reason, albatrosses produce babies only every other year (just like some penguins).

The prion is a very small, blackish-blue bird with a blue bill. Inside the bill is a kind of screen door, used to filter out the food as the prion swims along, bill open, slurping up krill (shrimplike creatures) and other small crustaceans. The water then streams out from two little pouches on the sides of its jaw.

The skua is the hoodlum of the bird bunch. It nests near the penguin rookeries so that it can grab penguin eggs or a baby penguin when the parents aren't looking. The skua is large (several times larger than a seagull) and brown, and it has a hooked beak. It sometimes uses its wings as weapons; a skua can swat its wing hard enough to kill a person. Several cases of this are on record.

(Burying supplies under snow and ice keeps the fierce winds from scattering them.)

Scott, beginning from a point about 400 miles away, laid down fewer supplies per person and in depots that were farther apart, to save time. His ponies, however strong, were unsuited to polar temperatures, and several had already died during this period of preparation. Dogs are better for polar travel because they perspire only from their mouths. Ponies sweat through their skin (as we do). Their sweat typically freezes, encasing them in ice. This ice had to be removed regularly, and the ponies were always very cold.

Meanwhile, back in Europe, the British had heard what Amundsen was up to. They were appalled that that he had concealed his intention to reach the South Pole. Even the Norwegians weren't too happy about being kept in the dark. But as the first winter arrived, interest in the race grew. Each group of men used the win-

NP RA 01141

Amundsen at camp in Antarctica.

Pole on November 1. Within just a few days, he ran into trouble. His motorized sledges had to be abandoned—the motors froze in the icy cold. More ponies died, too. At about this time, Amundsen was some 200 miles closer to the pole than Scott. When Amundsen achieved a new "farthest south," 82 degrees 20 minutes south latitude, he wrote this in his journal, which would be the basis for his book:

> We had a great piece of work before us that day: nothing less than carrying our flag farther south than the foot of man had trod. We had our silk flag ready; it was made fast to two ski-sticks and laid on Hanssen's sledge. I had given him orders that as soon as we had covered the distance to 88 degrees 23 minutes S., which was Shackleton's farthest south, the flag was to be hoisted on his sledge. It was my turn as forerunner, and I pushed on. There was no longer any difficulty in holding one's course; I had the grandest cloud-formations to steer by, and everything now went like a machine. First came the forerunner for the time being, then Hanssen, then Wisting, and finally Bjaaland. The forerunner who was not on duty went where he liked; as a rule he accompanied one or other of the sledges. I had long ago fallen into a reverie—far removed from the scene in which I was moving; what I thought about I do not remember now, but I was so preoccupied that I had

ter season to improve their equipment, work with the dog teams, and pack up their food. Then they had to wait for spring when they could go to the South Pole. (No one attempts long-distance exploration in Antarctica during the winter—that would be only a race to death.)

The Antarctic spring finally arrived, and it was time to race! On October 20, 1911, Amundsen started for the South Pole. Dogs dragged the sledges with the men on skis behind, guiding the dogs. Their pace was brisk and efficient. Scott headed out for the South

Some of the dogs on the Amundsen expedition: Mikkel, Reven, Elise, and Masmas.

was some way in advance of the others, so that I had time to pull myself together and master my feelings before reaching my comrades. We all shook hands, with mutual congratulations; we had won our way far by holding together, and we would go farther yet—to the end.

We did not pass that spot without according our highest tribute of admiration to the man, who—together with his gallant companions had planted his country's flag so infinitely nearer to the goal than any of his precursors. Ernest Shackleton's name will always be written in the annals of Antarctic exploration in letters of fire. Pluck and grit can work wonders, and I know of no better example of this than what that man has accomplished.

The Journey Continues

During the first month of his journey Amundsen discovered and named the Queen Maud Mountains, in honor of Norway's queen. These turned out to be part of the vast Transantarctic Mountain Chain. He also rescued two of the men in his group who had fallen into crevasses while crossing glaciers. Amundsen and his men finally came upon a section of ice that was crumpled into hundreds of dangerous crevasses. The ice was very dangerous, especially because

entirely forgotten my surroundings. Then suddenly I was roused from my dreaming by a jubilant shout, followed by ringing cheers. I turned round quickly to discover the reason of this unwonted occurrence, and stood speechless and overcome.

I find it impossible to express the feelings that possessed me at this moment. All the sledges had stopped, and from the foremost of them the Norwegian flag was flying. It shook itself out, waved and flapped so that the silk rustled; it looked wonderfully well in the pure, clear air and the shining white surroundings. 88 degrees 23 minutes was past; we were farther south than any human being had been. No other moment of the whole trip affected me like this. The tears forced their way to my eyes; by no effort of will could I keep them back. It was the flag yonder that conquered me and my will. Luckily I

a heavy, thick fog prevented the men from seeing very well. But they all managed to safely cross the area. Although they faced some dangers, Amundsen and his men enjoyed the trip, and even commented that skiing in Antarctica was just like skiing back at home in Norway. Amundsen's party had made good progress during the first month of their journey. The South Pole was now less than 100 miles away.

Things did not go so well for Scott. He and his crew encountered terrible blizzards, lost the rest of the ponies, and had to man-haul the heavy sledges along with the dogs. (They didn't have enough dogs for the animals to pull the sleds all by themselves.) Dragging 200-pound sledges behind them, they climbed up and over the Beardmore Glacier. The men were exhausted—and they were falling behind Amundsen by about 3½ miles every day. As they had planned earlier, some of Scott's men turned back in two stages, so they could act as a support party later. Scott and four of his men, on the polar plateau now, soon reached a point 150 miles from the South Pole.

Neither Scott nor Amundsen knew where the other was. By the time Amundsen reached 88–89 degrees south, he and his men began looking around constantly. Would they see Scott and his men on the horizon? Had their rivals already reached the South Pole? Could the British Union Jack already be flapping in the

breeze there? Amundsen had no way of knowing that Scott was actually many miles away.

On December 15, 1910, Amundsen won the race to the South Pole. Here's what he wrote in his journal about this momentous occasion.

At three in the afternoon a simultaneous "Halt!" rang out from the drivers. They had carefully examined their sledge-meters, and they all showed the full distance—our Pole by reckoning. The goal was reached, the journey ended. I cannot say though I know it would sound much more effective—that the object of my life was attained. That would be romancing rather too bare facedly. I had better be honest and admit straight out that I have never known any man to be placed in such a diametrically opposite position to the goal of his desires as I was at that moment. The regions around the North Pole—well, yes, the North Pole itself—had attracted me from childhood, and here I was at the South Pole. Can anything more topsy-turvy be imagined?

We reckoned now that we were at the Pole. Of course, every one of us knew that we were not standing on the absolute spot; it would be an impossibility with the time and instruments at our disposal to ascertain that exact spot. But we were so near it that the few miles which possibly separated us from it could not be of the slightest importance. It

was our intention to make a circle round this camp, with a radius of twelve and a half miles (20 kilometers), and to be satisfied with that. After we had halted we collected and congratulated each other.

The Victorious and the Vanquished Journey Back

Amundsen wanted to make absolutely sure that he and his party were indeed at the South Pole. There, using a sextant, they spent three whole days recording the sun's altitude in the sky, verifying and signing each other's measurements. They skied off 10 miles to the north, south, east, and west, and then at angles to join those four points into a square. This is called "boxing the Pole." Even if their measurements weren't exact, they knew that the South Pole had to be somewhere in that box. Amundsen really covered his bases. They left four notes for Scott to inform him that they had made it to the South Pole, saluted Norway's flag, then began the trek back.

Amundsen and his crew found all their depots on the way back and were able to eat well. On January 26, 1911, they reached their base hut, ending a round trip of some 1,400 miles in just over three months. Every man had survived. The remarkable voyage would lead

Amundsen's ship, the *Fram*.

people to claim Amundsen the most skilled polar explorer of all time. Amundsen and his crew were overjoyed at their success. They headed to Tasmania to send a cable home, telling their country that they had won the race to the South Pole.

Meanwhile, Scott and his men faced serious trouble. Out on the ice, they were cold and dehydrated. Their diets were very low in vitamin C, and the men showed signs of having scurvy. They also lacked vitamin B, which can affect mental function, including judgment. When they finally reached the South Pole, they were discouraged instead of elated: there was the Norwegian flag. They knew that Amundsen had beaten them.

Scott decided to continue to race on the way back, however. He hoped that he could still be the first to cable home the news that he had reached the South Pole. So his new goal was to reach New Zealand.

But, by the time they were about 300 miles away from their base hut, Scott and his men knew they were in deep trouble. They were cold, ill, and starving. Every time they reached one of their depots, they found that most of their heating and cooking fuel had vaporized—they hadn't sealed the storage canisters well enough. Without fuel, they couldn't melt enough snow for drinking water and, unable to create heat overnight, they were cold every minute of every day. Hunger also weakened them. They had not stored enough food in their depots.

Scurvy began to plague them even more intensely. In the later stages of this disease, the skin itself begins to break down. Old scars open up and bleed. Scott and his men experienced this as well as frostbite. The men who had left earlier so that they could assist the travelers at the end of the journey never arrived with their dog team. Two of the five men in Scott's group died. In a raging blizzard, stuck in tents and unable to search for their last depot, Scott ended his South Pole expedition with these journal entries:

Monday, March 19. Lunch. We camped with difficulty last night and were dreadfully cold, till after our supper of cold pemmican and biscuit and half a pannikin of cocoa cooked over the spirit. Then, contrary to expectation, we got warm and all slept well. Today we started in the usual dragging manner. Sledge dreadfully heavy. We are 15½ miles from the depot and ought to get there in three days. What progress! We have two day's food but barely a day's fuel. All our feet are getting bad—Wilson's best, my right foot worst, left all right. There is no chance to nurse one's feet till we can get hot food into us. Amputation is the least I can hope for now, but will the trouble spread? That is the serious question. The weather doesn't give us a chance—the wind from N. to N.W. and −40 degrees temp, to-day.

Wednesday, March 21. Got within 11 miles of depot Monday night; had to lay up all yesterday in severe blizzard. To-day forlorn hope, Wilson and Bowers going to depot for fuel.

Thursday, March 22 and 23. Blizzard bad as ever—Wilson and Bowers unable to start—to-morrow last chance—no fuel and only one or two of food left—must be near the end. Have decided it shall be natural—we shall march for the depot with our effects and die in our tracks.

Thursday, March 29. Since the 21st we have had a continuous gale from W.S.W. and S.W. We had fuel to make two cups of tea a piece and bare food for two days on the 20th. Every day we have been ready to start for our depot 11 miles away, but outside the door of the tent it remains a scene of whirling drift. I do not think we can hope for any better things now. We shall stick it out to the end, but we are getting weaker, of course, and the end cannot be far. It seems a pity, but I do not think I can write more

R. Scott

For God's sake look after our people

He and his two remaining men died.

One month after leaving Antarctica on the *Fram*, Amundsen arrived in Tasmania. From there he sent a cable to Europe, in which he made his claim as the first person to reach the South Pole. To repay expedition debts, he immediately began a lecture tour and rushed to finish his book. He was in the United States on his lecture tour when Scott's fate was finally discovered and his diary found. The diary not only made Scott a legend and a hero for his endurance, but a glorious failure, too.

One thing is certain: because Amundsen kept his quest for the South Pole a secret, he was not the cause of Scott's hasty preparation, nor was he to blame for his rival's unfortunate choices regarding supplies and transportation. Although many people believed that Amundsen had behaved deceitfully by keeping his journey to the South Pole a secret, most considered him as a hero and a celebrity once he claimed victory in the great race to "farthest south."

Amundsen's adventures did not end at the South Pole. Later he became a skilled pilot. Amundsen wanted to be the first person to *fly* over the North Pole, and, although he reached 87 degrees 44 minutes north latitude, his first attempt at this was unsuccessful. Shortly after Amundsen's failed attempt, Admiral Richard E. Byrd (see Chapter 13) claimed to have succeeded in flying over the North Pole. (Most researchers now doubt that he did so.) Still, Amundsen tried again. This time he did fly over the North Pole. With Admiral Byrd's claim in doubt, it's possible that Amundsen had indeed achieved another first.

Assessing Wind Speed

When Antarctic explorers such as Amundsen were racing for the Pole, they felt the wind speed directly, right on their faces. But, at base camp, investigating the wind from *inside* the shelter can be a very good idea. In order to try this activity, you will need several consecutive windy days.

1. Tape the box shut, then cut off both ends, leaving a four-sided tunnel.
2. Reinforce all of the tunnel's edges with electrical or packing tape so that the box feels sturdy.

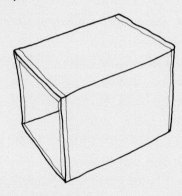

3. Using the wire clipper, cut the coat hanger to make one piece of wire that is 3 inches longer than the width of the open end of the box.
4. Poke two holes in the cardboard box, each at a place that is ½ inch in from the open end and ½ inch below the top of the box. These holes

---

Materials

Adult supervision required	Box cutter or very sharp knife
Electrical tape or packing tape	Wire clipper
Medium-sized cardboard box (larger than a shoe box but smaller than a computer printer box)	Wire coat hanger, straightened
	Aluminum foil
	Scissors
	Clear tape
	Marker

need to be at exactly the same positions on both sides of the open end.

5. Push the wire through the first hole, straight across the opening and inside the box, and then through the second hole. Bend the wire ends down on both sides, to make small hand-holds.

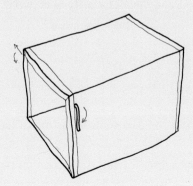

---

6. Cut the aluminum foil to make a curtain. Using the long, straight part of the wire as the "curtain rod," fold the foil securely but loosely over the rod. The foil curtain should swing freely into the box, about an inch above the bottom of the box. Trim the bottom and sides of your curtain if necessary to allow it to swing freely.
7. Using clear tape, tape the foil onto the wire at the top. Tape a smooth edge around all four sides of the front of the box opening, so that the foil can move as freely as possible.

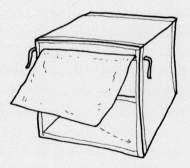

8. To calibrate the wind box, lightly push in the foil and see how far in it will go. Mark this on the side of your box as the end of your wind speed dial. Now push in the foil half as far. Make a mark on the side of the box in this place. Now push in the foil half as far and make a mark here.

9. Connect the marks on the side of the box and draw an arc. Cut the arc so the edge of the foil is visible through the slice.

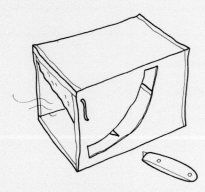

10. Contact the National Weather Service or a local television station to get today's wind speed.
11. Take the box outside into an open area and face it into the wind. See how far the foil curtain moves back. Mark this on the side of the box and using a marker, write this number representing the wind's force on the side of the box.

12. Perform steps 9 and 10 on several days with different wind conditions until you have several numbers on your calibration arc.

13. Place your wind box in an open area near a window, with the calibration arc facing inside your house and with the opening facing west (the most common direction for the wind in our hemisphere). Make sure that the box isn't just facing the house, which would block the wind. Now you can read the wind speed from the comfort of home!
14. As necessary, move the box to face the wind in whatever direction it is coming from.

Beaufort Scale

Wind Force	Wind Observed	Wind Speed	
		Miles per hour	Kilometers per hour
0	smoke rises straight up	less than 1	less than 1.6
2	leaves rustle on trees	4–76	.5–11
4	loose paper pieces blow around	13–18	21–29
6	opened umbrellas are difficult to hold	25–31	40–50
8	walking against the wind is very difficult	39–46	63–74
10	trees are uprooted	55–63	89–102

111

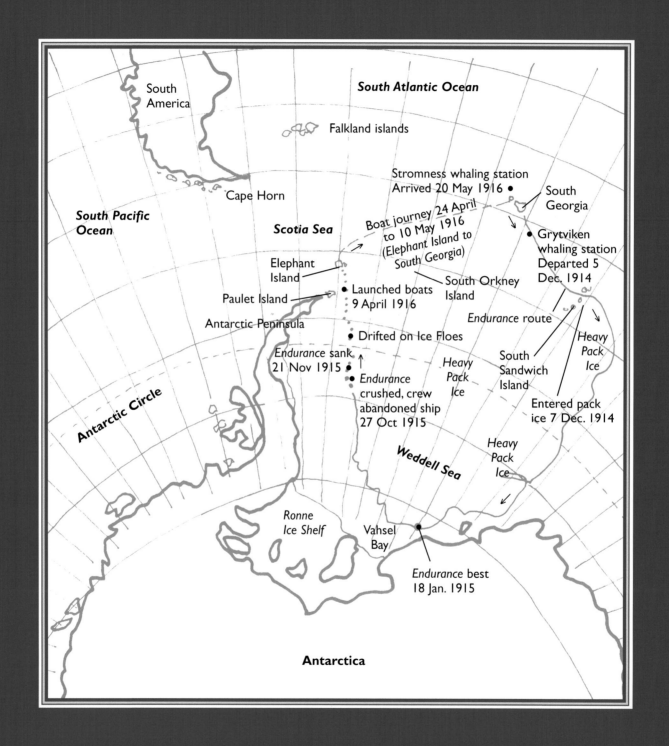

12

Ernest Shackleton Attempts to Cross Antarctica, 1914–1916

This map shows the route of the Shackleton expedition, by sea in the *Endurance* and then by small boat as he strived to save all of his men.

As the early 1900s unfolded, Antarctic exploration had become more vigorous, and even more countries joined the adventure. Both European and South American countries claimed territories for whaling and for empire-building—and to prevent other nations from claiming the land instead. Here are a few examples.

A major whaling station, Grytviken, was established in the harbor of the South Georgia Islands off Antarctica's northwest coast. It housed Norwegian ships and crews for months at a time. This base operated until the 1960s.

The German Erich Dagobert von Drygalski discovered, explored, claimed, and named Wilhelm II Land.

The kind of shoreline that Shackleton saw.

Norwegian whaling captain Carl Anton Larsen, Scottish explorer William Bruce, and French adventurer Jean-Baptiste Charcot also explored the continent.

Amundsen and Scott raced to the South Pole in 1911–1912.

Ernest Shackleton Joins the Race

British explorer Ernest Shackleton (1874–1922) first joined the Antarctica adventure in 1901–1908. He was part of Captain Robert Scott's unsuccessful first attempt, in 1901, to reach the South Pole. During the expedition, Shackleton developed scurvy and couldn't complete the journey. Far from dampening his adventurous nature, however, his experience in Antarctica only fueled his desire for adventure.

Shackleton led his first expedition in 1907–1908, accompanied by both ponies and dogs for transportation. He chose the Ross Sea area that James Clark Ross had discovered as his launch point, and he set a double goal: to discover both the Magnetic South Pole and the Geographic South Pole. Achieving these goals would take a lot of effort, because both poles are well inland, and an explorer would have to traverse a lot of icy, dangerous land to get to them. By 1908 Shackleton and his men reached 85 degrees 55 minutes south latitude. They photographed themselves near the British flag they'd

Shackleton's ship, the *Endurance*, trapped and in grave danger of being crushed.

planted there. But they were running low on food. The mountainous altitudes of the polar plateau also weakened them with almost paralyzing headaches.

On January 9, 1908, Shackleton recorded this in his journal:

Our last day outwards. We have shot our bolt, and the tale is latitude 88 degrees 23 minutes South, longitude 162 degrees East. The wind eased down at 1 A.M., and at 2 A.M. we were up and had breakfast. At 4 A.M. started south, with the Queen's Union Jack, a brass cylinder

A resting elephant seal.

Icebergs

Large icebergs can weigh as much as 10 million tons, and about 90 percent of an iceberg can be underwater.

we only did two hours' march in the afternoon and camped at 5:30 P.M. The temperature was minus 19 degrees Fahr. Fortunately for us, our tracks were not obliterated by the blizzard; indeed, they stood up, making a trail easily followed. Homeward bound at last. Whatever regrets may be, we have done our best.

Though he reached 88 degrees 23 minutes south latitude, Shackleton turned around and headed home. He was less than 100 miles (161 kilometers)—less than two degrees—from the Geographic South Pole, but he and his men were so weak that continuing on might have killed them all! A week later, on the way back, three of his men reached the Magnetic South Pole at 72 degrees 25 minutes south latitude and 155 degrees 16 minutes east longitude. It, too, was at a treacherously high altitude on the polar plateau.

Once back in Britain, Shackleton wrote a book titled *The Heart of Antarctica*, gave lectures, and turned his ship, the *Nimrod*, into a museum. The money he received from each of

containing stamps and documents to place at the furthest south point, camera, glasses, and compass. At 9 A.M. we were in 88 degrees 23 minutes South, half running and half walking over a surface much hardened by the recent blizzard. It was strange for us to go along without the nightmare of a sledge dragging behind us. We . . . took possession of the plateau in the name of His Majesty. While the Union Jack

blew out stiffly in the icy gale that cut us to the bone, we looked south with our powerful glasses, but could see nothing but the dead white snow plain. There was no break in the plateau as it extended toward the Pole, and we feel sure that the goal we have failed to reach lies on this plain. We stayed only a few minutes, and . . . hurried back and reached our camp about 3 P.M. We were so dead tired that

these ventures went to pay back the loans he'd taken to finance the expedition.

Shackleton Makes History

Shackleton's next expedition made him famous, although the goal he achieved during the voyage was not the one he had sought. Roald Amundsen had already reached the South Pole by then, so Shackleton set a new goal for himself: to be the first to cross Antarctica on foot with dogsleds. This would involve a trip of about 1,500 miles over land from the Weddell Sea to the Ross Sea. Five thousand men volunteered for the journey. Shackleton took fewer than 30 of them, as well as 69 dogs and a cat named Mrs. Chippy, on his ship, the *Endurance*. An excellent photographer named James Francis Hurley also accompanied him. Hurley's photographs helped make this expedition even more famous. Shackleton and his crew left Britain in August 1914.

It wasn't long before the Antarctic winter closed in on them. The weather they encountered was bad, even by Antarctic standards: the men faced winds with speeds of 100 miles (161 kilometers) per hour and temperatures as low as −70° F (−57° C). Icebergs as large as football fields surrounded them. The men could actually hear the ice thicken around them (some recalled that it sounded like a big slurp). In this, the winter of 1915, at 74 degrees south latitude, the *Endurance* became trapped in the

An elephant seal can make a lot of noise.

ice of the Weddell Sea. It remained there all winter.

Shackleton was known for treating his men with concern and respect. All winter, the men played football on the ice, read books, and played chess. They also organized races and games with the dogs, building them "dogloos" on the ice to sleep in. All of them worked hard, then relaxed at evening sing-alongs. The sounds of a banjo and a gramophone, a very early record player, filled the ship. The scientists among them observed the stars, weather, and wildlife. The conditions were difficult, especially when the ice moved them away from their destination, but they kept active to keep their spirits up. After spending 326 days trapped in the ice, the boat was finally freed of its icy prison as spring arrived and the weather warmed a bit.

A king penguin on a warm summer day by the shore.

Orcas, also called killer whales, come to the surface to breathe.

Unfortunately, the warming weather worsened their situation. The shifting ice twisted, shivered, lifted, and ultimately crushed their ship. The men had barely decided to abandon their ship before they found themselves fighting for their lives. Grabbing the lifeboats and some supplies, they left the ship and set up an encampment on an immense ice floe some 300 miles (484 kilometers) from land. Shackleton knew that he had to give up his goal of crossing Antarctica on foot when, in late November, their ship actually sank. Now Shackleton had a new goal: to save the life of every one of his men.

After months and months of living on the ice floe, eating foods such as blubber and penguin livers, and drifting some 600 miles (968 kilometers), the clutch of ice finally loosened. It was time to try and get away! They launched their lifeboats and threaded through icebergs and treacherous storms for seven days. Finally they reached a place called Elephant Island, the only haven around. It was April 15, 1915. Exhausted, they managed to land on the rocky beach. Elephant Island was large but empty of food, except for more penguins and seals. Shackleton knew that, although they were temporarily safe, no search party would know to look for them there. If he was going to save his men, he desperately needed to somehow reach civilization.

As the ship's carpenter constructed a hut out of one of the lifeboats, Shackleton prepared a radical plan: using the other lifeboat, the *James Caird*, he would attempt to reach Grytviken, the whaling station at South Georgia. This was approximately 800 miles (1,290 kilometers)

Crabeater seals are sleek, efficient swimmers.

away, over open ocean—and it was winter in Antarctica. Since his navigation could not be perfect—sextants don't work well on overcast days—Shackleton knew that he could miss the island entirely (even though at its narrowest point it is 30 miles [48.4 kilometers] wide and more than 100 miles [161 kilometers] long). If that happened, Shackleton and the men who went with him would only sail to their deaths over more open ocean, and the men who stayed behind on the island would die as well.

Shackleton chose five crewmembers to make the journey with him and promised the remaining men that he would return for them. He and the five crewmen pushed off into the sea, and soon faded from the remaining men's view.

After 15 days at sea, they finally spotted South Georgia. Weak from exposure and hunger, they barely had the strength to make it to shore. Luckily, the hurricane winds they were battling subsided just before completely destroying the boat. Unfortunately, they found them-

selves on the opposite side of the island from the whaling station!

To get to the whaling station, Shackleton and his men crossed mountains, glacier crevasses, and snowfields, trekking 30 miles across the island. Finally, they heard the sound of a whistle at the whaling station. That whistle was probably the most beautiful sound Shackleton and his men had ever heard, because it meant that they were almost there!

When the Norwegian whaling captain on duty learned that his visitor was none other than Shackleton, he wept with joy. Everyone in Europe thought that he and his men had all died.

Finally, after three different tries in three different boats, Shackleton made it back to Elephant Island to rescue his remaining crew. It was August 30, and they had almost given up hope for good. When the men saw a boat in the distance, they all rushed to the shore. Shackleton immediately counted their distant forms. "They're all there!" he said. Not one of his crew had died.

Back in Britain, Shackleton wrote a book, titled *South*, about the experience, and he planned yet another Antarctic expedition, this time on the ship *Quest*. During that voyage he and his crew stopped at South Georgia again on the way south. There Shackleton suffered a heart attack and died. He was buried on this island that had helped to save his life and the lives of his men so many years ago.

Shackleton's men ready to push off the small boat the *James Caird*.

How Wet Is Snow?

Polar explorers such as Ernest Shackleton all knew how important the moisture content of snow can be, and how much that varies. Very wet snow can be sticky, making it difficult to move in. Dry, powdery snow is easier to move in, but because it has very little moisture, quite a lot of it has to be melted in order to make just a little bit of drinking water. This activity requires that you either have several consecutive days of snowy weather or access to a large area that has a variety of snow conditions, such as a ski resort.

1. Draw a line across the top of the long side of a piece of graph paper. Mark off the line in 33 small segments of roughly equal width. Label them as ⅛ cup, ½ cup, ⅛ cup, ½ cup, and so on. Set this aside.
2. Take the containers, their lids or foil covers, and the knife outside. Fill one container with very powdery snow. Using the knife, scrape off the excess snow at the top so that the container is exactly full but not overflowing. Seal it. Bring it inside and place it near a sunny window.
3. Repeat the process with three of the remaining containers, filling one container with each of the following: snow that's a little less powdery than what was put into the first container; snow that just barely sticks to the bottom of your boots

Materials
Pencil
1 sheet of 8½ × 11-inch graph paper
5 empty containers, all with wide openings and of the same size (soup cans are fine but somewhat larger containers will be easier to work with)

Lids to fit the containers or foil to seal them
Table knife
5 small pieces of paper
Clear tape
Measuring cup
5 differently colored markers

(perhaps from under a tree); and slushy snow (perhaps from a driveway). Fill the last container with water. Be sure to cover the containers as soon as you've leveled off the snow in them, to prevent evaporation. As you fill each container, bring it inside and place it next to the others.
4. Make labels for your containers. On each small piece of paper, write the kind of snow (or water) used to fill each container and the location where you scooped it up. Tape each label to its container.
5. Let the containers sit overnight. The next day, open each container to see if its snow has melted to water. If not, seal them all up again and wait longer.
6. When the snow in all of the containers is completely melted, pour the water from the container marked "very powdery snow" into the measuring cup. Check to see how much water the snow made. Using one of the colored markers, place a big dot on your graph next to the right number for that amount of water. At the bottom of the page, using the same marker, write down the name of that snow condition and where you found it. Pour out the water and dry the measuring cup.
7. Repeat this process with each of the remaining containers, using a different colored marker to record the information of each type of snow on your graph.

13

Admiral Richard E. Byrd Is First to Fly Over the South Pole, 1929

By the time Shackleton died in 1922, the "heroic age," which pitted humans against the forces of nature, had given way to more high-tech advances in polar travel. The airplane, especially, became the modern way to explore. A new generation of explorers took to the skies. Lincoln Ellsworth of America and George Hubert Wilkins of Australia flew together over huge sections of Antarctica in three stages in 1939. But it was Admiral Richard E. Byrd (1888–1957), an American naval officer, who became the first and most famous polar aviator. He aimed for more than just Antarctic exploration; he wanted to fly over the South Pole itself.

Weddell seals keep a breathing hole open, year-round.

Byrd began first with Arctic exploration, flying over Greenland in 1925. Soon afterward, in 1926, he decided to fly over the North Pole. Taking off from Spitsbergen (the Norwegian island in the high Arctic), Byrd and his colleague Floyd Bennett took a nonmagnetic sun compass, a device to measure wind drift, and a sextant with them so that they could find the North Pole and establish the latitude they reached. Already, Byrd had sold "newsreel rights" to a company prepared to film their flight. (Newsreels were the short news films shown in movie theaters before the main feature. At this time television had not yet been invented, so this was the only way that people "saw" the news.) Their flight to the North Pole took 16 hours and, in the process, they lost the sextant. Without this device, it became difficult for them to determine the precise measurement of their positions. Though Byrd claimed that they had flown over the North Pole, most people believe that, at best, they got only within 20 miles of it, and, at worst, they were more like 150 miles off. (His achievement was disputed mainly because people didn't think he could have reached the Pole in 16 hours.) Nevertheless, the handsome and dashing explorer captured the interest and admiration of people all over the world. Story after story was written about him and his daring adventures. Parents named their sons after him. Richard E. Byrd was on his way to becoming a legend.

Byrd's next goal was to explore the Antarctic by plane and to fly over the South Pole. On this expedition, which was privately funded, Byrd planned to make detailed aerial maps and meteorological observations of the area, and claim Antarctic land for the United States. Byrd set off for Antarctica in late 1928. Among the people in his expedition was 19-year-old Paul Siple, a Boy Scout who had won the privilege of coming on the voyage in a nationwide Boy Scout contest.

Siple's duties during the long months of the journey included helping to train the dog teams, studying penguins and seals, and helping out in the kitchen. (Others in the group made weather observations, moved equipment from ship to base, protected men and machinery from the cold, prepared for possible rescue, and the like.) Siple's adventure in Antarctica lasted for 14 months. Here is part of the application the Boy Scout wrote when he entered the contest:

A blue-eyed shag looks at the snow.

Why I Feel That I Would Be of Service to the Expedition

My several years of experience in Scouting have played a large part in making me physically fit, mentally awake and morally straight. I am proud of the fact that I am an Eagle Scout with twenty-one required Merit Badges and thirty-eight additional ones.

My Sea Scouting experience extends over a period of five years, during which time I have worked up to the Able Sea Scout Rank. I have maneuvered in small boats on Lake Erie.

During the last six years I have officially spent thirty-five weeks of actual camping and have been on innumerable overnight hikes. I have done at least four weeks of winter camping, spending the majority of the nights in shelters of my own making, in snow storms and very inclement weather. From this experience I feel somewhat prepared to withstand Antarctic conditions. I have passed my Hiking Merit Badge and do considerable walking every day. In this respect I am sure I would not be a detriment to the expedition.

In connection with the passing of the Astronomy Merit Badge, I did considerably more work than was required as Astronomy is a hobby of mine.

I am prepared to face the hardships and would certainly appreciate any consideration you may give me.

Paul A. Siple

Byrd's plane took off from his Antarctic base near the Ross Ice Shelf on November 28, 1929. By November 29, Byrd and the three adult crewmembers who accompanied him had indeed flown over the South Pole and back. Paul Siple and the rest of Byrd's 42-man crew stayed behind at the base, helping them to take off and to land. Byrd returned to America a hero and a celebrity. And America wanted more.

Paul Siple later wrote a book about his experience, *A Boy Scout with Byrd*, which was published when he was 22 years old. He grew up to be an Antarctic scientist. Paul Siple died in 1968.

Byrd Takes Flight Again

Byrd's second expedition to Antarctica is even more famous than his first, mostly because of the dramatic danger he encountered. He left the

Antarctica as seen from the air.

United States in 1933, setting up a base camp in Antarctica called Little America. A correspondent from CBS Radio accompanied Byrd and his crew on this trip, and, in February of 1934, Byrd participated in the first radio broadcast from Antarctica, titled *CBS Radio from Little America*. Radio was still a rather new technology in those days, and programs were rarely transmitted from such faraway places.

In March 1934 Byrd settled down to overwinter at an inland hut called Advance Base, recording weather observations and details on the aurora australis, or southern lights. He wanted to be the first person ever to spend the winter alone in Antarctica. He planned to read books and listen to music on the newly invented phonograph (a music record player), and he had a radio to communicate with the Little America base, which was 123 miles (198 kilometers) away. Byrd had flown in ahead of time with several of his men to set up his weather station. The hut itself and many supplies were brought in by tractor, and this marked the first time tractors were used so extensively in Antarctica. (His men warmed the engines' oil by blowtorch each morning to get the tractors to start.)

Once set up alone in the hut, Byrd ordered his men not to return for him until spring, even if they lost radio contact—it would be just too dangerous to come during the winter.

Within a few weeks, Byrd was already having difficulties. He wrote in his journal:

At times I felt as if I were the last survivor of an Ice Age, striving to hold on with the flimsy tools bequeathed by an easy-going, temperate world. Cold does queer things. At 50 degrees below zero a flashlight dies out in your hand. At –55 degrees kerosene will freeze, and the flame will dry up on the wick. At –60 degrees rubber turns brittle. One day, I remember, the antenna wire snapped in my hands when I tried to bend it to make a new connection. Below –60 degrees cold will find the last microscopic touch of oil in an instrument and stop it dead. If there is the slightest breeze, you can hear your breath freeze as it floats away, making a sound like that of Chinese firecrackers. As does the morning

The Aurora Australis

The *aurora borealis*, also called the northern lights, creates a famous sky show in the Arctic. The *aurora australis*, or southern lights, is its Antarctic counterpart. Byrd recorded many observations of the southern lights, noting how often they occurred and how much of the sky they covered. Every other South Pole explorer who has witnessed this phenomenon is struck by its exquisite dance of light across the dark sky. Multicolored light sweeps, plunges, swirls, shimmers, and pulses—it's as though the whole sky were alive.

These auroral lights occur because of a completely natural electrical interaction between the sun and the Earth's atmosphere. The sun, a thermonuclear ball of fiery hot gas in motion, experiences magnetic storms every so often in which its natural magnetic fields twist and swirl. Immense amounts of energy flare out from them and stream through the solar system. Some of this energy reaches our atmosphere. Our planet has its own magnetic field (far weaker than the sun's). The Earth's magnetic field is stronger in Antarctica and the Arctic because the magnetic lines of force come down to the ground at both ends of the planet. These magnetic lines are invisible, but they surround our planet.

As energy from the sun plunges toward the magnetic poles it bombards the Earth's atmosphere and collides with atoms and molecules there. This produces the fantastic light shows at both poles.

The farther north you live in the northern hemisphere, and the farther south you live in the southern hemisphere, the more likely you are to see these amazing sights. Check out www.space weather.com on the Internet for information on when the sun is experiencing a magnetic sub-storm. A day or two after this date is when the aurora will appear!

dew, rime coats every exposed object. And if you work too hard and breathe too deeply, your lungs will sometimes feel as if they were on fire.

Cold—even April's relatively moderate cold—gave me plenty to think about.

Ice regularly encased the hut's door hatch, and Byrd had to chip at it for hours before could go in or out. But he was still walking outside for several hours every day as well as recording dozens of weather and auroral observations daily. One day he saw rings of a rainbow around the moon, which shimmered for a full five minutes. The rainbow was caused by sunlight (reflected from the moon) splitting into all the colors of the spectrum as it passed through high-atmosphere ice crystals. (These ice crystals separate light into its components the way glass does in a prism.) Winter was deepening. In his journal Byrd wrote:

> Thus the coming of the polar night is not the spectacular rush that some imagine it to be. The day is not abruptly walled off; the night does not drop suddenly. Rather, the effect is a gradual accumulation, like that of an infinitely prolonged tide. Each day the darkness, which is the tide, washes in a little farther and stays a little longer; each time the day, which is a beach, contracts a little more, until at last it is covered. The onlooker is not conscious of haste. On the contrary, he is sensible of something of incalculable importance being accomplished with timeless patience. The going of the day is a gradual process, modulated by the intervention of twilight. You look up, and it is gone. But not completely. Long after the horizon has interposed itself, the sun continues to cast up a pale and dwindling imitation of the day. You can trace its progress by the glow thrown up as it makes its round just below the horizon.

On April 17 the sun vanished for the winter and wouldn't reappear for almost six months.

One of Admiral Byrd's camps in Antarctica.

Byrd realized that his three main dangers were accidentally starting a fire in the hut, getting lost, and illness or injury. Soon he was indeed developing headaches, pain in his eyes, and feelings of depression. It was −72° F (−58° C) outside, and the hatch continued to stick regularly. He wrote:

> I've been trying to analyze the effect of isolation on a man. As I said, it is difficult for me to put this into words. I can only feel the absence of certain things, the exaggeration of others. In civilization my necessarily gregarious life with its countless distractions and diversions had blinded me to how vitally important a role they really did play. I find that their sudden removal has been much more of a wrench than I had anticipated. As much as anything, I miss being insulted every now and then.

Make a Water Thermometer

Admiral Byrd and other polar explorers had thermometers in their huts. It's possible to make a very basic thermometer in your own kitchen, without using dangerous chemicals such as mercury to measure extremely low temperatures. Instead, you can use water to measure rising temperatures, and learn some interesting science as you do it.

Materials

Adult supervision required	Cork that fits tight at bottle's mouth
Masking tape	Screwdriver
Ruler	I clear straw
Pen	Food coloring
I clean 10-ounce plastic soda bottle	Piece of paper
Clear tape	Heatproof pan that has sides at least 4 inches high
Sharp knife	

1. Tear off a 4-inch piece of masking tape. Using the ruler and pen, make a mark on the tape every quarter inch, for a total of 16 small marks (like those on a ruler). Number them from I to 16 right on the tape.
2. Place the bottle on its side and stick the 4-inch-long piece of tape along the side of the bottle lengthwise, with the number I mark being nearest the bottle's bottom. The other end of the tape should stretch up toward the top of the bottle but not reach the top.
3. Using the knife, cut the cork in half lengthwise.
6. Using the screwdriver, hollow out a tunnel in one half of the cork, so that the straw will fit between the two halves of the cork.
7. Fill the bottle halfway with water. Add a tiny amount of food coloring, just enough to tint the water.
8. Put the straw in the bottle and hold it so that the bottom of the straw is almost, but not quite, at the bottom of the bottle, and not leaning against the sides. Use clear tape to tightly tape the two halves of the cork together and around the straw. Then tightly stuff the cork into the top of the bottle so that air can't get into the bottle.
9. Measure the water level in the bottle and mark down on a sheet of paper how high it is. Label this "Observation 1."
10. Place the bottle in the pan, and add very hot water from the faucet, up to about one-third of the height of the bottle. Watch the water rise in the straw. Measure the water, then mark down how high it rises as "Observation 2."
11. Turn on the burner to heat the water even more, but not to the boiling point. Measure the water, then mark down that level too, as "Observation 3."
12. Turn off the burner and let the water cool. Now think about what happened here. As the water in the pan got hotter, its heat warmed the air inside the bottle. The air there expanded and, unable to get out, pushed down on the water in the bottle. When the water couldn't compress any more, it moved up the straw. So the higher numbers show higher temperature inside the bottle.

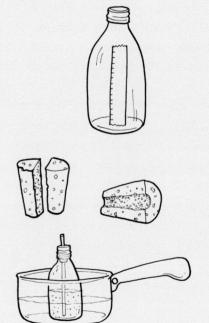

A Weddell seal rests with her pup.

Byrd continued to conceal his plight in his regular communication with Little America, even though he was usually so nauseated that he could not eat without vomiting. The two camps communicated by Morse code (a series of long and short taps makes up each word), not by voice, so it wasn't too hard to hide his struggles. Periods of brief lucidity alternated with three long periods of extreme weakness, pain, and depression. He moved in slow motion, if at all, and kept the toxic heater off for hours at a time, turning it back on only when he felt he was close to freezing to death. After a while, the regular radio broke, and he had to use the crank-up auxiliary radio. He suffered in silence and isolation.

The men back at the Little America base began to suspect that Byrd was in trouble, but they were all well aware of his strict instructions not to leave their base to check on him. They stayed at Little America and waited for word from Byrd.

Byrd, meanwhile, stayed alive, but barely. One day, it was −83° F (−46° C) degrees below zero in the hut, and at this temperature large patches of skin were peeling off his face.

As winter was ending, the men at Little America, who were by now very worried about Byrd, tried four times to travel to him, but four times they had to turn back. Daylight was just beginning to return to Antarctica in August when they reached him. Amazingly, he was still alive. Byrd was rescued! But, weakened

His problems worsened. Byrd actually passed out, and when he returned to consciousness, he was intensely nauseated and almost too weak to move. He was barely able to turn off his gas heater, which he suspected might be his problem. Overcome by dizziness and a terrific pain in his ear, he was barely able to move. By the time his heater had been off for 12 hours, he had eaten no food for 36 hours and was very cold and weak. He fainted again. When he returned to consciousness he wrote farewell letters to his family and to the crew at Little America. Byrd had come to believe that he was dying of carbon monoxide poisoning from the heater because its ventilation vent kept freezing solid. That prevented the noxious exhaust from escaping outside. He didn't want the crew to risk their lives to save his, so he didn't contact them about his illness.

Volleyball is a popular sport among scientists and staff in Antarctica.

Life on Land in Antarctica

In addition to lichens—flat plants that live on and under rocks—Antarctica is home to mites and midges (both tiny insects), two species of flowering plants (which grow low to the ground with tiny flowers), and 39 species of nesting birds. None of these exist near the area where Byrd spent his solitary winter.

and discouraged, he was never the same man again.

Later, Byrd made three more trips to Antarctica, though he never attempted another period of solitude there. One trip lasted from late 1939 to early 1940. Another, a naval expedition in 1946–47, involved a 13-ship convoy and crew to make aerial photos of parts of the coastline. This had never been attempted before. And in his last trip, in 1955–56, he helped to organize the upcoming venture called the International Geophysical Year, in which scientists from all over the world were to study the continent.

During his Antarctic career, Byrd achieved many important things. He and his men were responsible for the discovery of the most southerly fossils (found farther south than anyone ever had found fossils before), as well as lichen, bacteria, and molds on the continent, and for the establishment of extensive meteorological records. He also established airplane flight as a regular part of Antarctic exploration, and he made the continent and its resources a well-known part of the world. He also named several areas of Antarctica, including Marie Byrd Land, which he named for his wife.

Communicating by Morse Code

Admiral Byrd used this form of communication when he overwintered in the hut alone. The scientific principle here is that a metal stylus—or tapper—is activated by an electromagnetic current to spell out words via a code made up by dots and dashes.

A gentoo penguin with an egg.

Materials	
2 "Morse Code Experiment" kits from Edmund Scientific (cost under $10 apiece—see	www.scientificsonline.com) A friend in a nearby house or family member in a nearby room

1. Assemble both kits, following the instructions provided with them.
2. Learn the code with your friend or family member. Keep a cheat sheet near your machines, in case you need to refresh your memory as you communicate.
3. Find the first three sentences of Admiral Byrd's writing that begins "Thus the coming of the polar night . . ." without telling your partner what sentences you have selected. Send them to your partner by Morse code.
4. Have your partner write down what he or she thinks you've said, then see how well the message was communicated. Now imagine how hard this would be to do if you were all alone and near death in an ice-cold hut!
5. Pretend that you are in Antarctica. Write your own sentence or paragraph about being there. You might describe what the weather is like, or what your next exploration or science experiment will be. Send this message to your partner by Morse code, and see how well it is communicated to him or her.

Morse Code

Alphabet		Numerals	Punctuation Marks
a .-	n -.	1 .----	apostrophe .----.
ä .-.-	ñ --.--	2 ..---	colon ---...
å .--.-	o ---	3 ...--	comma --..--
b -...	ö ---.	4 ....-	hyphen -....-
c -.-.	p .--.	5	parenthesis -.--.-
ch ----	q --.-	6 -....	period .-.-.-
d -..	r .-.	7 --...	question mark ..--..
e .	s ...	8 ---..	quotation mark .-..-.
é ..-..	t -	9 ----.	
f ..-.	u ..-	0 -----	*Distress signal (SOS)*
g --.	ü ..--		...---...
h	v ...-		
i ..	w .--		
j .---	x -..-		
k -.-	y -.--		
l .-..	z --..		
m --			

14

Scientist Bill Green Studies Antarctic Lakes, 1980–1994

As explorers discovered more and more of Antarctica, countries started to fight over who owned land there and who had a right to use its natural resources. After many years, most of these conflicts were resolved, but some—especially those that involve protection of Antarctica's environment—continue to this day.

The 1950s were marked by a period of international tension called the Cold War. To prevent these tensions from spreading to the Antarctic continent, President Dwight D. Eisenhower proposed an international agreement stating that Antarctica should be used for peaceful purposes only. Twelve nations—Argentina, Australia, Belgium, Chile, France, Great Britain, Japan, New Zealand,

An emperor penguin stands on the snow with Mt. Erebus, an Antarctic volcano, behind.

Norway, South Africa, the Soviet Union, and the United States—quickly agreed and cooperated to write a tready. The Antarctic Treaty was signed in 1959 and went into full effect in 1961.

The agreement was also designed to create a good basis for discussions and agreements among all countries of the world. As of today, all of these countries have signed the treaty: Argentina, Australia, Austria, Belgium, Brazil, Bulgaria, Chile, China, Cuba, The Czech Republic, Ecuador, Finland, France, Germany, Great Britain, Greece, Hungary, India, Italy, Japan, The Netherlands, New Zealand, North Korea, Norway, Papua New Guinea, Poland, Peru, Romania, Russia, South Africa, South Korea, Spain, Sweden, Uruguay, and the United States. More countries are expected to sign it, too, as time goes on.

Tourism, whaling, and scientific expeditions continued to increase in the 1950s. Some people wondered how Antarctica would be affected by the sudden presence of all these people and their activities. After all, Antarctica had been completely uninhabited by humans for thousands of years! As early as the late 1940s, discussions focused on controlling whaling. These discussions led to the formation of the International Whaling Commission to regulate the activity, but it was not until the mid-1980s that whaling in Antarctica was actually forbidden. Unfortunately, by then Antarctica's whale pop-

ulation had already been seriously lessened, and the blue whale had been hunted to near extinction. Whaling in Antarctica continues to be forbidden, but enforcing this ban is sometimes difficult.

In addition to protecting its whales, many people wanted to save the seals, birds, and other wildlife in Antarctica. Not everyone was interested in helping the environment, but some progress toward protecting these animals was made. Other people set up volunteer programs to clean up the garbage, sewage, empty fuel containers, and the like at the continent's research bases.

By the late 1950s, science was the major activity in Antarctica. The first International Geophysical Year, 1957–1958, brought together scientists from 67 countries to study everything about Antarctica, from its astronomy to its zoology. More research stations were built. And, in 1969, the first women participated in Antarctic scientific expeditions, at bases where private facilities could be set up for them.

Tourism in Antarctica kept growing, however, and scientists continued to worry about its effects (as well as the effects of the 68 bases that had been built) on Antarctica's wildlife. Of even more concern, however, was a new environmental issue: protecting the oil, natural gas, and mineral resources of Antarctica. Drilling for these resources was prohibited (by "voluntary restraint") in 1977. These days it is too expen-

A rock hopper penguin doesn't mind hopping over a few rocks!

sive to search for Antarctic oil, drill it, and then ship it out—it's cheaper for companies to do this elsewhere in the world. This way of thinking, however, could change at any time.

By the early 1980s, as more and more scientists, tourists, and small groups of adventurers came to visit Antarctica, an effort was made to persuade the world, especially those nations that had land claims there, to make Antarctica a protected "world park." (Various scenarios were put forward for this, most involving no further land claims, drilling bans, etc.) Environmental organizations and some environmentally minded public figures lobbied the United States

Congress for this and received media attention for their efforts, but they did not achieve their goal. But this project could be revived at any time.

During the summer of 1980, many scientists worked in Antarctica. One of them was Bill Green, a geochemist from Miami University in Ohio. He later wrote a book, titled *Water, Ice & Stone: Science and Memory on the Antarctic Lakes*, about his research. Though many scientists have written about Antarctica, none has done so with more grace and insight.

Green conducted his research with different groups of scientists over a total of 14 summer months "on the ice" between 1980 and 1994. Green's research focused on five unusual Antarctic lakes. Unlike most of the rest of the continent, these lakes are not frozen solid. In fact, the water at the bottom of one of them was measured at 77° F (25° C)!

These very unusual lakes are in the McMurdo Dry Valleys, a 1,500-square-mile section of Antarctica where three valleys lie among glaciers. The valleys are dry because mountains block ice from flowing into them and high winds and low snowfall keep the ground quite bare. The McMurdo Dry Valleys area has been like this for about four million years. Green calls it an "improbable Eden of ice and stone."

Green and his colleagues travel to the lakes from their base at McMurdo Station on Ross Island, about 70 miles from the Dry Valleys.

A World Park? Lobby for It!

You can help protect Antarctica's wildlife, land, and resources, even if you live thousands of miles away from the continent. Here are some ways you can do this. You can get the names, mailing addresses, and e-mail addresses of the people and organizations mentioned here at your local library or on the Internet.

1. Write a letter to the president of the United States and to your state's senators and members of Congress. Tell them why you want to protect the environment in Antarctica and ask them to help do this with laws and other regulations. Maybe you'd like to ask them to make Antarctica a World Park!

2. Write a letter to the National Science Foundation's Antarctic Division, which operates the United States science bases in Antarctica. In your letter, describe what you are doing to protect the continent (such as writing letters to the president) and why you are interested in Antarctica. Try to be specific. Maybe you love penguins and want to make sure that their home is safe and protected. Perhaps you want to travel to Antarctica someday to climb a glacier. Write about the thing that you like the most about Antarctica and ask them to help protect it. You might also ask them for more ideas on what you can do to help. Here is the mail address and the Web site for the center:

Antarctic Resource Center
U.S.G.S. National Center
12201 Sunrise Valley Drive
MS 515
Reston, VA 20192
http://usarc.usgs.gov/

3. Write more letters asking people to help protect Antarctica! You can write letters to your local newspaper, to your favorite magazine—even to environmental organizations that are already working to protect Antarctica. You can find the names and addresses of many such organizations at your local library or on the Internet. Here is just one:

Sierra Club
85 Second St., 2nd Floor
San Francisco, CA 94105-3441
E-mail: information@sierraclub.org

Scientists work in many places in Antarctica.

Meteorites

In an area near the McMurdo Dry Valleys, almost 8,000 meteorites lie on the ice! They didn't all fall right here.

For millions of years, Antarctica's glaciers have scooped up and pushed the meteorites here from various places. Many more of these space rocks, which look like slightly burned stones, probably were shoved right into the Antarctic Ocean. But, here in the McMurdo Dry Valleys, strong winds finally blew away a lot of the glacial ice to reveal these rocks that fell out of the sky. No place else on the planet has a meteorite collection like this.

They are flown by helicopter to the various lakes, where they live in tents and conduct experiments and make scientific observations for weeks at a time. Since the sun never sets during the Antarctic summer, they also have time to hike and have fun in the fiercely beautiful area.

The five lakes—Lake Miers, Lake Vanda, Lake Hoare, Lake Fryxell, and Lake Bonney—each lie under a lid of ice. This top layer of ice can be as thick as 13 feet (4 meters). The Onyx River, which flows only for about six weeks in summertime, washes melted glacier water into Lake Vanda. The other lakes sometimes have smaller streams feeding into them, too.

In these lakes there are no fish or any other large creatures. The inhabitants are algae, bacteria, and yeasts. The lakes also have puzzling water layers. Among other things, the bottom layer—which can be 200 feet (61 meters) deep—is usually the warmest. This is the opposite of most other lakes in the world, in which top water layers, being closer to the sun, are warmer.

Green, like most scientists, focuses his knowledge and curiosity on a specific question. He studies to better understand the chemistry of the lakes' water. Yet he never loses sight of the big picture of how water moves through and transforms our planet. This global water cycle includes rivers washing rock and debris into the world's oceans and lakes; water evaporating up

Some scientists have a working camp in the Dry Valleys, west of the Ross Ice Shelf in southern Antarctica.

Old Ice

Polar researchers drink water melted from ice near their research bases. This ice formed when snowfalls from long ago compacted—an ice cube in Antarctica can easily be made of 800-year-old ice.

to make rain, which then falls back down onto the land and sea; and water evaporating to leave sea cliffs and rocks inland. While this is happening, air is also moving throughout the system. Animals on the planet breathe in oxygen and breathe out carbon dioxide. Plants take in carbon dioxide and create oxygen. The oxygen never runs out for us and the carbon dioxide doesn't poison us or run out for the plants. This

great circle, called the "global carbon cycle," is the basis of Green's studies. Our lives depend upon it.

It is easy to think of water as having nothing in it, or maybe to think of it as just a combination of hydrogen and oxygen. But natural lake water has plenty of other elements in it, and they affect the way these lakes and the oceans operate within the water and carbon cycles. Out-

side of the polar regions, for example, corals and other sea creatures absorb a lot of the carbon. They use it to make reefs and shells, releasing oxygen back into the atmosphere. These sea creatures are so numerous that, when they die, their shells (made of calcium carbonate, a mineral containing carbon) have been gradually forced together and moved to land, over millions of years, to make limestone, marble, and other types of rock. In this way, the sea creatures affect the carbon cycle on land as well as in the ocean.

In fact, if our planet didn't have just the right amount of carbon in the air (in the form of a related molecule, carbon dioxide), the atmosphere would absorb too much or too little energy from the sun. This would make our planet either an inferno, like the planet Venus, or a frozen ball, like the planet Mars.

Bill Green and other scientists research Antarctic lakes to see how the major and minor

Bill Green and a colleague gather scientific data.

natural chemicals in the lake water—especially the tiny amounts of calcium, magnesium, sodium, potassium, bicarbonate, chloride, and sulfate, as well as trace elements such as carbon and manganese—dissolved there, and how these chemicals fit into the big picture of the water and carbon cycles. Antarctica is a good place to study this. Not only has it not been highly polluted, like most of the rest of the planet has, but the continent is almost like the entire earth was hundreds of millions of years ago, in the days before there were any plants at all on the land and the world's carbon cycle was just beginning.

To do their work, scientists in Antarctica, or anywhere, need scientific theories (ideas), plans, and equipment. In his book, Green describes how he and his colleagues planned to test the water of Lake Miers. It took a whole week to get all the equipment—from drills to filters to flow meters—working properly in such a difficult research location. Once everything was ready, Green and his colleagues transported the equipment to the lake, where it would remain for a year. Using the instruments, Green and the others collected information about the water flow at various levels of the lake, drilling through the ice to probe the lower layers. After they had gathered their first measurements about the amount of salt in the lake, they left everything to freeze in place.

Their next stop was Lake Vanda, a lake about four miles long and a mile wide. It is also 250 feet deep, and its basin was hollowed out by a huge glacier millions of years ago. Green and the others retrieved the equipment they'd left at Lake Vanda the year before. (The equipment collected data about the lake throughout the year.) Green and the others almost fell into Lake Vanda while removing the drill, and they discovered that the top water layers under the lake's ice are clean enough to drink. About 170 feet (52 meters) down, however, the water becomes very salty, and is full of more calcium than any other lake has ever been known to contain. Still, it is one of the clearest lakes in the world.

Green and his colleagues thought hard about this strange phenomenon, and they came up with theories about what might have caused the lakes to become like this. Green is especially interested in how lakes, as compared to oceans, deal with all the trace metals that enter them. Trace metals get into our lakes and oceans in many ways— they wash into bodies of water, dissolve from rocks already in the water, and spout up from the ocean floor in the lava of volcanoes. It's all part of the earth's water and carbon cycles.

In his book, Green wrote about his work that he did back at home, between trips to Antarctica. He tested water samples from the lakes in his lab, read a great deal, and discussed the puzzle of Antarctica's lakes with scientists who study the water chemistry of the ocean. He also put together his own data, starting with how different the Antarctic lakes are from each other.

Back in Antarctica, Green and his colleagues visited Lake Hoare and the stream that feeds it with meltwater from the nearby Canada Glacier. They listed the trace metals found and measured in the lake water: manganese, iron, cobalt, nickel, copper, zinc, cadmium, and lead. None of these is considered a pollutant—tiny quantities of the metals, like those found here, occur naturally in the earth's waters. But these metals have been washing into lakes and oceans for millions of years. If they just stayed there in the water, our lakes and oceans would be soupy with these metals. But Green and the others found only trace amounts of these in the lakes of Antarctica. Was something taking metals *out* of lakes and oceans as well? If so, what could be removing them? Or were the metals turning into something else in the water?

Back at Lake Vanda again, Green discovered that the manganese found in the lower layers of the lake was, in fact, changing, and that this change is part of the carbon cycle:

At fifty-five meters, manganese was being reduced, it was gaining electrons from all of the decaying carbon down there; you could see that in the profile. It was as clear as anything. I began to construct a little story about the manganese. I didn't know whether it was true or not, but I knew eventually we could test it and find out. That was the way science worked. You wrote a story. It was pure imagination bounded by a few, usually weak, constraints. Then you tested it, saw whether the world out there could really abide your notions of what was so. Usually it could not. So you tried again and again until you got it. Until you had something that might actually be so.

As Green wrote in his book, the work of scientists and of explorers is not always what we might think it is:

Somehow we have come to think of science, at its best, as discovery. We think of the scientist as someone like James Clark Ross, who, setting sail upon the waters of the unknown, comes, perhaps at great sacrifice, into the Land of Light; who nudges his ship through ice floes and howling winds into the safe harbor beneath the mountain; who gestures and points and names everything within view. This is discovery: coming nobly and with great fortitude and perseverance and with no little wit and energy upon that which already exists, upon that which, however hidden or far away, is already with us. Just as Ross came upon these islands and ice shelves and seas, so too did Dalton, we think, come upon his atoms. Rutherford upon his nucleus, Henry Frank upon his flickering clusters deep within the structure of water, and Robert Garrels upon his cycles of carbon and oxygen endlessly turning through geologic time. We think of the scientist as we think of Ross and Scott, as the discerners and revealers of what is actually out there in the capacious provinces of the world; of what is waiting passively to be discerned and revealed. We think of the scientist, at best, as a discoverer.

Next, Green and the other scientists helicoptered to Lake Fryxell, which is about 60 miles (97 kilometers) from Mt. Erebus, Antarctica's most famous volcano. The scientists saw no lava coming from the volcano in the distance, but a plume of steam whiskered out of its summit as they worked. In this lake, Green's team found that primitive bacteria, living deep down in the lake, were sopping up some of the carbon. Green began to wonder if the algae found in these lakes absorbs metals as well.

By 1994 Green figured out that it was the manganese particles in the water that were responsible for removing carbon particles from the lakes and oceans. Green discovered that manganese is one of nature's cleaners! This can be seen clearly only in Antarctic lakes, but it applies elsewhere. As Green puts it:

> There is a kind of conspiracy at work.... It is worldwide and, as far as we know, benevolent. In every lake and ocean, in every parcel of atmosphere, there is a cleansing that tempers the Earth, that drags it back from squalor, that countervails its self-undoing. Metals pour into the lake, but the lake removes them. Metals pour into the sea, but the sea is not full. The volcanoes breathe sulfur and chlorine, but the rains and winds carry them to earth transformed.

Too much dissolved metal in the waters of the world would poison us. But if we didn't have enough of these metal traces in our waters, all life would gradually die. Because metals are linked to the carbon cycle and help to speed it along, an imbalance of them would mean that there would not be enough carbon dioxide for the plants, which in turn would mean not

Bill Green is happy to work in Antarctica!

enough oxygen for us. So these tiny amounts of natural metals in water are very important.

You have probably heard of greenhouse gases and how we now have too much of them up in the atmosphere. (They get there as we burn coal for power plants, drive cars, and so on.) Carbon dioxide is a greenhouse gas. If it

damages life on our planet, it will be because we have overwhelmed the power of the carbon cycle. This cycle is keeping us alive and healthy now.

So, though Bill Green's research sounds complex, it has global significance.

Create an Edible Map of Antarctica

It is probably safe to say that, no matter how hungry Antarctica's explorers became during their expeditions, few (if any) ate their own maps! Here's a way to make an edible map that any explorer would enjoy feasting on.

1. Preheat the oven according to the cookie dough package directions.
2. Lightly grease the cookie sheet with the butter or oil.
3. Using a rolling pin, roll the cookie dough flat onto the cookie sheet.
4. Using the table knife, cut the edges of the dough to create the shape of Antarctica. Use the atlas or map for reference.
5. Using the cookie dough scraps that were cut away, create some of Antarctica's natural features, such as its volcanoes and mountain ranges. Press your features into the flat cookie dough, placing them where the real features would be. Use the topographical map for reference.
6. Bake your continent according to the cookie-dough package directions. When it's done,

Materials

Adult spervision required
1 roll premade sugar cookie dough (available in the refrigerated section of most grocery stores)
1 teaspoon of butter or cooking oil
Rolling pin
Table knife
Atlas with a topographical map of Antarctica

Cookie sheet
1 can ready-to-use vanilla icing
$1/2$ cup granulated sugar
Several (8–20) black jelly beans
White marshmallows
1 thin pretzel stick
Blue construction paper
Black marker

remove the cookie sheet from the oven. Turn off the oven and let your cookie continent cool.

7. Add even more features to your cookie continent. Spread a thin layer of icing all over it, except where the Dry Valleys would be (use the topographical map for reference). Sprinkle sugar onto the icing. Now you have ice and snow. Put a black jelly bean on top of your volcanoes to represent smoke. (Use icing to secure it to the cookie.) You can create glaciers with big swoops of icing, and the coastal ice sheets with extra sugar sprinkled onto the icing there. Cut the remaining jelly beans into small pieces and add them to the Dry Valleys area of your cookie continent to indicate the meteorites that have collected there over millions of years. Place marshmallows on your continent to represent research bases. You can come up with more ideas for fun, tasty things to add as Antarctic features.

8. Place the pretzel stick in your continent to represent the South Pole itself.
9. Cut and place blue construction paper around the edges of your continent, all the way out to the edge of the cookie sheet. This will represent the ocean.
10. Using the black marker, draw some whales, seals, penguins, and other creatures on the blue paper.
11. Enjoy eating Antarctica!

Epilogue

Tourists, adventurers, scientists, controversy, and global warming all continue to be part of the Antarctic picture.

Though tourism remains expensive, approximately 20,000 people arrive in Antarctica on cruise ships every year. Most of these tourists visit the Antarctic Peninsula or Ross Island, where they are taken to shore on small boats for short excursions. Tourists are told to "take nothing but pictures and leave nothing but footprints." Yet even a footprint on a small mat of Antarctic moss can take many years to disappear as the plant recovers. And penguins can become stressed by having to avoid the tourists' paths. The cruise ships themselves emit fuel and other pollutants. Even a single plastic bag blown over the side of a ship can carry organisms to shore that were never there before. These new organisms will probably interfere with Antarctica's own native organisms. Concerns such as these make some environmental organizations want to limit tourism. Such groups include the Sierra Club, Greenpeace, and the Antarctic Project.

A few adventurers come to Antarctica each year to explore its glaciers and other features. None are allowed to bring dogs, in case illnesses might be transmitted from them to local wildlife.

Some visitors ski across different sections of the continent. Others climb mountains and glaciers or even skydive over the land. Not all of these adventurers are men. Ann Bancroft and Liv Arneson, for example, recently became the first women to ski across Antarctica. Adventurers are always looking for something unique to do, and sometimes they get into trouble in Antarctica. Many have required elaborate and expensive rescue efforts, mounted by airplane under the direction of the United States government's National Science Foundation (NSF). These rescues leave behind pollution in the form of exhaust fumes from airplanes, for example.

The NSF manages Antarctica's entire American scientific effort, which is quite large. Hundreds of scientists do research in Antarctica every year, and they need a large support staff of mechanics, cooks, pilots, and others. The bulldozers, fuel cans, and sewage from the research bases pollute Antarctica as well.

The environmental dangers created by all three of these groups is a concern to many people. Antarctica is a powerful but also a fragile place.

The continent is also key to understanding global warming and the role of people in the development of this condition. Right now some of Antarctica's ice shelves are breaking off and gradually melting. In 2002 a section of the Ross Ice Shelf that was 47 miles (75.6 kilometers) by 4.6 miles (7.4 kilometers) wide broke off from the mainland; the section began slowly to erode, and its location is being monitored. Other large sections of ice have broken off elsewhere in Antarctica. Since 1995, several thousand square miles of ice shelf have vanished from the continent's edges, either by breaking off or melting. Most of this has been in Antarctica's warmest area, the Antarctic Peninsula. Broken-off ice from an ice shelf does not raise the level of the world's oceans—it was floating to begin with. But as glaciers melt, the water is added to the oceans, causing them to rise. A rise of only two inches in the oceans' waters would cause the waterline on shores all over the world to rise anywhere from 9 to 36 feet!

In some sections of Antarctica, however, the glaciers are thickening, not melting, and snowfall is increasing. Since Antarctica is such an immense place, weather conditions are not uniform across the continent. It is still not clear if the climate there is gradually but steadily warming. One thing is certain, though: Antarctica is still the world's coldest place.

Selected Answers

Chapter 3
A Puzzle and a Theory About January Temperatures
A city's latitude is only part of the reason for its average temperature. Two other factors play a huge part in determining how cold or warm the average temperature of a city is.

A city that sits on a large body of water probably has a warmer average temperature than you would expect if you looked only at that city's latitude. Throughout much of the fall, oceans, even the Arctic Ocean, are warmer than the air that surrounds them. Some of the seaside cities listed in this activity border an ocean that freezes very late or not at all. These places have what is called a *maritime climate*. Cities that lie inland have what is called a *continental climate*. These cities have much colder winters than the cities by the oceans.

Another factor of a city's average temperature involves elevation. The higher the elevation, the colder it is, so a city that is higher up on a plateau or mountain is colder than one that is near sea level. The last factor, latitude, is indeed part of the answer, but only part of it.

Chapter 6
Arctic Weather
What kind of weather phenomenon almost never occurs in the Arctic? Although "rain" is a good guess, that's not the answer (it does rain very occasionally during the summer). The answer is lightning. Lightning happens when a mass of cold air meets a mass of warm air—and there are no warm air masses in the Arctic!

Chapter 9
How Long Does It Take to Freeze?
Foods that are low in water content, such as bread, freeze quickly. When they defrost, they taste just fine. Foods that are liquid (very high in water content) develop ice crystals. They taste OK, but not great, when completely defrosted. Foods that are high in both protein and water, such as eggs, freeze relatively slowly, and they don't taste very good when they're thawed and cooked.

Glossary

Age of Discovery: a period, from the 1400s to the 1600s, during which many people explored uncharted areas of the world.

Aurora australis: a light phenomenon that occurs in the Earth's southern hemisphere (also called the southern lights).

Aurora borealis: a light phenomenon that occurs in the Earth's northern hemisphere (also called the northern lights).

Antarctic Convergence: The zone, roughly circular and at about 50 degrees to 63 degrees south latitude, where the ocean around Antarctica meets warmer ocean water.

Backstaff: a navigational instrument formerly used at sea to measure the elevation of the stars and other bodies in the night sky above the horizon.

Barometer: an instrument used to assist in forecasting weather by determining the pressure of the atmosphere.

Blubber: the fat of whales and other large marine mammals.

Chronometer: a timepiece that is designed to keep time with great accuracy.

Circumnavigate: To go completely around, by water.

Circumpolar: surrounding or found in the area of the North Pole or the South Pole.

Compass: a device that indicates direction (north, south, east, and west).

Continental climate: the climate of inland areas.

Cross-staff: a navigational instrument formerly used at sea to measure the altitude of the sun.

Daguerreotype: an early photograph, produced on a silver or silver-coated copper plate.

Dark Ages: the primitive period in history from about A.D. 476 to about 1000.

Depot: a place for storage of supplies.

Esquimaux: a name used by early explorers to describe the native peoples of the Arctic.

Ethnographer: a scientist who studies the ways of life of native people.

Fjord: a narrow inlet of the sea that flows between steep slopes, glaciers, or cliffs.

Floe: a large sheet of ice that floats on the surface of an ocean or other body of water.

Geographic North Pole: the northernmost point of the earth, at 90 degrees north latitude.

Geographic South Pole: the southernmost point of the earth, at 90 degrees south latitude.

Global warming: an increase in the average temperature of the Earth's atmosphere.

GPS (Global Positioning System): A method of using satellites high in Earth's atmosphere to allow anyone with a receiver to discover the exact latitude and longitude of where that person is located. Some cars are equipped with GPS these days.

Harpoon: A barbed spear used in hunting whales and other large marine animals.

Hibernation: a period of very deep sleep experienced by some animals during the winter.

Hyperboreans: the mythical early inhabitants of the Arctic.

Ice Age: a prehistoric time when ice covered most of the earth.

Iceblink: a glare in the sky over an ice field.

Inuit: the native people of the Arctic (formerly called Eskimos).

Kittiwake: a cliff-nesting gull.

Latitude: the location of a place north or south of the Earth's equator, measured through 90 degrees.

Lichen: a type of fungal plant that grows on rocks and other solid surfaces.

Longitude: the location of a place east or west of an imaginary north–south line called the prime meridian.

Magnetic North Pole: the point at which the Earth's shifting magnetic lines of force converge in the northern hemisphere.

Magnetic South Pole: the point at which the Earth's shifting magnetic lines of force converge in the southern hemisphere.

Maritime climate: the climate of areas that are near large bodies of water.

Meltwater: water derived from melting ice or snow.

Mirage: a deceptive image caused when light is bent by temperature differences.

Mutiny: An uprising in which sailors try to take command of the ship away from the captain.

Narwhal: a whale found in the Arctic.

Northwest Passage: A route that ships can take between Europe and Asia by going through the Arctic.

Outlawry: a punishment used by the Vikings in which convicted criminals were banished from society for a period of time.

Overwinter: to stay through the winter.

Pack ice: a mass of sea ice formed by the crushing together of other forms of ice.

Pemmican: a dense mixture of beef, fat, and other ingredients eaten by native peoples and explorers.

Polynya: an area of open water in sea ice.

Pressure ridge: a ridge formed by slabs of ice pushed against and over each other.

Renaissance: a movement in Europe, from the 14th to the 17th century, that focused on the arts, literature, and science.

Rookery: a breeding or nesting ground of birds.

Rune: the characters of the Runic alphabet, which was used by the Vikings and other peoples from about the third to the 13th century.

Scurvy: a disease caused by a lack of vitamin C.

Sextant: an instrument used for navigating by measuring the elevation of the sun and stars above the horizon.

Ship's log: a record, kept daily by the captain of a ship, that describes occurrences during an expedition.

Sledge: a strong, heavy sled.

Sun dogs: rings around the sun caused by reflection and refraction of ice crystals high in the atmosphere.

Whaling: the occupation of killing whales and selling their meat and other parts.

Web Sites

Admiral Richard Byrd

www.south-pole.com/p0000107.htm

Provides a lengthy biography on Byrd and all his voyages to the South Pole, and features photographs of many of the ships he used in his travels. Includes links to pages on Roald Amundsen, Robert Scott, and Ernest Shackleton.

Age of Discovery

www.mariner.org/age/menu.html

Offers links to informational pages on Viking explorers, Viking ships, methods of navigation, maps, charts, Henry Hudson, James Cook, and more.

Antarctica

www.coolantarctica.com

Features information on virtually every aspect of Antarctica. Includes pages on individual explorers, animals, and other subjects, as well as photos.

www.antarcticconnection.com

Offers information and products related to Antarctica, including Antarctic news and South Pole weather, maps, videos, books, and more.

www.bartelby.com/151/c8.html

Features maps, a brief history of Antarctica, and information about the continent's geography, inhabitants, government, economy, communications, transportation, and military.

Antarctic Animals

www.enchantedlearning.com/school/Antarctica/Animalprintouts.shtml

Provides information on Antarctica and the animals that live there, as well as photographs of some of these animals.

Antarctic Explorers

www.south-pole.com

Features an index of the major Arctic and Antarctic heroes of discovery, with biographies and reading lists.

Arctic Studies Center

www.mnh.si.edu/arctic

Focuses on Vikings and the North Atlantic Saga. Features information on Arctic wildlife and Inuit clans. This site is linked to the National Museum of Natural History.

Captain James Cook

www.south-pole.com/p0000071.htm

Biography of the explorer with details of his Antarctica voyages.

Discovery of the North Pole

www.northpole1909.com

The discovery story of Peary and Henson, and includes new evidence about the race.

Frederick A. Cook Society

www.cookpolar.org

History of Frederick Cook, polar exploration links, and polar research today.

Fridjof Nansen

www.fni.no/christ.htm

Features a biography of Fridtjof Nansen's life, including a large section on the voyage of the *Fram*.

Geography Trivia

www.odci.gov/cia/ciakids/games/geography/index.html

Features quizzes and maps of the whole world, with special sections about the Arctic and Antarctica. Test your knowledge on this site.

Glory and Honor

http://learning.turner.com/tntlearning/glory/inuits.html

This site's perspective is through the eyes of Matthew Henson; it includes sections on the Inuit and how they helped, the race to the pole, different expeditions, a time line, and list of links to other Arctic exploration sites.

Hudson Bay Company

www.gov.mb.ca/chc/archives/hbca

Includes documents, maps, photos, and film of the history of the Hudson Bay Company.

Introduction to Exploration of the Northwest Passage

www.collections.ic.gc.ca

Offers a history of the Northwest Passage and the search for it, as well as information about explorers including: Roald Amundsen, John Franklin, Edward Parry, John Davis, and Henry Hudson.

Matthew Henson

www.matthewhenson.com

Provides a list of books related to the North Pole, articles on Matthew Henson, and on Peary's expedition to the North Pole.

National Geographic

http://magma.nationalgeographic.com

A number of multimedia presentations on Antarctica, including a 360° panorama from the South Pole, and pictures from the top of Mt. Erebus.

National Science Foundation

http://quest.arc.nasa.gov/antarctica/background/NSF/

Includes general information on Antarctica, information on different research stations, as well as the National Anthem of Antarctica.

Roald Amundsen

www.mnc.net/norway/roald.html

Includes his biography, photos, and links to articles on him.

Sir John Franklin

www.ric.edu/rpotter/SJFranklin.html

Offers many links, as well as section on searching for his lost voyage and the fate of his voyage. Includes many images.

Through the Northwest Passage

www.users.voicenet.com/~jstewart/nwt/nwt.html

A photo essay of a voyage through the Northwest Passage. Includes pictures of places such as Davis Strait, Johansen Bay, and Barrow Strait. Includes links to other relevant sites.

The Vikings

www.bbc.co.uk/education/vikings

Discusses Viking invasion, Viking life, Viking beliefs, travel, trade, and exploration. Includes a time line and several games and other activities.

Wild Arctic Activities

www.seaworld.org/arctic/index.html

Through games, mazes, puzzles, and activities, become an Arctic expert. Includes vocabulary, polar profiles, and an Arctic word search.

Bibliography

Albanov, Valerian. *In The Land of White Death.* New York: Modern Library, 2001.

*Alexander, Caroline. *The Endurance: Shackleton's Legendary Antarctic Expedition.* New York: Alfred A. Knopf, 1998.

Arms, Myron. *Riddle of the Ice: A Scientific Adventure into the Arctic.* New York: Doubleday, 1998.

Boorstin, Daniel J. *The Discoverers: A History of Man's Search to Know His World and Himself.* New York: Random House, 1983.

Brody, Hugh. *The Other Side of Eden.* New York: North Point Press/Farrar, Straus and Giroux, 2000.

Byrd, Richard E. *Alone.* New York: G. P. Putnam's Sons, 1938.

Byrd, Richard E. *To the Pole: The Diary and Notebook of Richard E. Byrd, 1925–1927.* Columbus: Ohio State University Press, 1998.

Capelotti, P. J. *By Airship to the North Pole.* New Brunswick, NJ: Rutgers University Press, 1999.

Cook, James. *A Voyage toward the South Pole, and round the world. Performed in His Majesty's Ships the Resolution and Adventure in the years 1772, 1773, 1774, and 1775.* Adelaide: Libraries Board of South Australia, 1970.

Cookman, Scott. *Ice Blink: The Tragic Fate of Sir John Franklin's Lost Polar Expedition.* New York, John Wiley & Sons, 2000.

Delgado, James P. *Across the Top of the World.* New York: Checkmark Books/Facts on File, 1999.

De Poncins, Gontran. *Kabloona.* Alexandria, VA: Time-Life Books, 1941.

Ehrlich, Gretel. *This Cold Heaven: Seven Seasons in Greenland.* New York: Pantheon Books, 2001.

Fisher, David E. *Across the Top of the World: To the North Pole by Sled, Balloon, Airplane, and Nuclear Icebreaker.* New York: Random House, 1992.

Fisher, Dennis. *Latitude Hooks and Azimuth Rings: How to Build and Use 18 Traditional Navigational Tools.* Camden, ME: International Marine, 1995.

Franklin, John. *Narrative of a Journey to the Shores of the Polar Sea in the Years 1819, 20, 21, and 22.* Rutland, VT: Charles E. Tuttle, 1970.

Fredston, Jill. *Rowing to Latitude: Journeys Along the Arctic's Edge.* New York: North Point Press/Farrar Straus & Giroux, 2001.

Huntford, Roland. *Scott and Amudsen.* New York, Atheneum, 1984.

Keay, John, ed. *The Mammoth Book of Explorers.* New York: Carroll & Graf, 2002.

Landis, Marilyn J. *Antarctica: Exploring the Extreme, 400 Years of Adventure.* Chicago: Chicago Review Press, 2001.

Lopez, Barry. *Arctic Dreams: Imagination and Desire in a Northern Landscape.* New York: Charles Scribner's Sons, 1986.

Malaurie, Jean. *The Last Kings of Thule: With the Polar Eskimos as They Face Their Destiny.* New York: E. P. Dutton, 1982.

*May, John. *The Greenpeace Book of Antarctica: A New View of the Seventh Continent.* New York: Doubleday, 1988.

Mulvaney, Kieran. *At the Ends of the Earth: A History of the Polar Regions.* Washington DC: Island Press, 2001.

Nansen, Fridtjof. *Farthest North.* New York: Modern Library, 1999.

Nickerson, Sheila. *Midnight to the North: The Untold Story of the Inuit Woman Who Saved the Polaris Expedition.* New York: Tarcher/Putnam, 2002.

Norman, Howard, ed. *Northern Tales: Traditional Stories of Eskimo and Indian Peoples.* New York: Pantheon Books, 1990.

Officer, Charles, and Jake Page. *A Fabulous Kingdom: The Exploration of the Arctic.* New York: Oxford University Press, 2001.

Parry, William Edward. *Journal of a Voyage for the Discovery of a North-West Passage from the Atlantic to the Pacific.* London: John Murray, 1821.

Parry, William Edward. *Journal of a Second Voyage for the Discovery of a North-West Passage from the Atlantic to the Pacific.* London: John Murray, 1825.

Page, R. I. *Reading the Past, Runes.* Berkeley and Los Angeles: University of California Press/British Museum, 1987.

Rasky, Frank. *The North Pole or Bust.* Toronto: McGraw-Hill Ryerson Limited, 1977.

Ross, Sir James. *A Voyage of Discovery and Research in the Southern and Antarctic Regions During the Years 1839–1843, volume 1.* New York: Augustus M. Kelley, 1969.

*Siple, Paul. *A Boy Scout with Byrd*. New York & London: G. P. Putnam's Sons, 1931.

Sobel, Dava. *Longitude: The Story of a Lone Genius Who Solved the Greatest Scientific Problem of His Time*. New York: Walker, 1995.

Thayer, Helen. *Polar Dream: The Heroic Saga of the First Solo Journey by a Woman and Her Dog to the Pole*. New York: Simon & Schuster, 1993.

*Verne, Jules. *Twenty Thousand Leagues Under the Sea*. Hertfordshire: Wordsworth Editions Limited, 1992.

Wright, Theon. *Big Nail: The Story of the Cook–Peary Feud*. New York: The John Day Company, 1970.

Young, Steven B. *To the Arctic: An Introduction to the Far Northern World*. New York: John Wiley & Sons, 1989.

*Books appropriate for children

Credits

Page ii
Royal Geographic Society, London

Page x
Photodisc, Inc.

Chapter 1

Page 4
Iceland Tourist Board

Page 8
Iceland Tourist Board

Page 12
Iceland Tourist Board

Page 14
National Science Foundation

Page 16
National Science Foundation

Page 20
National Science Foundation

Page 21
National Science Foundation

Page 21 (sextant)
Vancouver Maritime Museum

Chapter 3

Page 28
National Science Foundation

Page 30
National Science Foundation

Chapter 4

Page 34
National Portrait Gallery, London

Page 35
National Science Foundation

Page 36
Toronto Reference Library

Chapter 5

Page 45
National Maritime Museum, London

Page 46
National Maritime Museum, London

Page 47
National Maritime Museum, London

Page 49
National Maritime Museum, London

Chapter 6

Page 54
Norsk Folkenmuseum

Page 57
Norsk Folkenmuseum

Page 59
Vancouver Maritime Museum

Page 61
Vancouver Maritime Museum

Page 62
Photodisc, Inc.

Chapter 7

Page 65
National Archives

Page 67
Bettmann/CORBIS

Page 77
Photodisc, Inc.

Chapter 9

Page 80
National Science Foundation

Page 82
National Portrait Gallery, London

Page 84
State Library of South Australia

Page 86
National Science Foundation

Page 87
National Science Foundation

Page 88
National Science Foundation

Chapter 10

Page 92
National Portrait Gallery, London

Page 94
National Science Foundation

Page 95
National Science Foundation

Chapter 11

Page 98
Norsk Folkemuseum

Page 101
Norsk Folkemuseum

Page 101
National Portrait Gallery, London

Page 103
National Library of Norway

Page 105
National Library of Norway

Page 106
National Library of Norway

Page 107
National Library of Norway

Page 108
National Library of Norway

Chapter 12

Page 114
National Science Foundation

Page 115
Royal Geographical Society, London

Page 116
National Science Foundation

Page 117
National Science Foundation

Page 118 (orcas)
National Science Foundation

Page 118 (king penguin)
National Science Foundation

Page 119
National Science Foundation

Page 120
Royal Geographical Society, London

Chapter 13

Page 122
National Science Foundation

Page 124
National Science Foundation

Page 125
National Science Foundation

Page 127
National Science Foundation

Page 129
National Science Foundation

Page 130
National Science Foundation

Page 131
National Science Foundation

Chapter 14

Page 132
National Science Foundation

Page 134
National Science Foundation

Page 136
National Science Foundation

Page 137
National Science Foundation

Page 138
Bill Green

Page 140
Bill Green

Index

150